For

From
About
James T. Whitehead

For
From
About
James T. Whitehead

Poems, Stories, Photographs, and Recollections

Edited by Michael Burns
Assisted by James S. Baumlin

Photographs by Bruce West

Moon City Press

Springfield, Missouri
2009

For inquiries contact
Moon City Press
Department of English
Missouri State University
Springfield, MO 65897

Cover photography:
"Burning Field, Mississippi" (front cover) and "The Road
Home, Mississippi" (back cover) by Bruce West,
copyright © 2009

Library of Congress Cataloging-in-Publication Data

For, from, about James T. Whitehead : poems, stories, photo-
graphs, and recollections.
        p. cm.
  Includes bibliographical references.
  ISBN 978-0-913785-15-7
  1. Whitehead, James T. I. Baumlin, James S. II. Burns, Michael,
  1953- III. Whitehead, James T.
  PS3573.H48Z65 2009
  811'.54--dc22
                                    2009000429

Contents

About Whitehead

From Whitehead

(selected and co-edited by Jessica Glover,
Eric Sentell, and Caleb Stokes)

For Whitehead

A Family Photo Album

MICHAEL BURNS

Preface
"When I Walked Into Big Jim's Office in March of 1979"

When I walked into Big Jim's office in March of 1979, he swiveled in his chair and faced me with one of his infamous scowls. "Burns," he said, "Where the hell have you been?" I told him I had gone home for my father's funeral. He got up out of his chair and put his hands on my shoulders. His look softened in the way it sometimes did, not a rare thing exactly but a moment many of us learned to count on and cherish. "Get your coat," he said.

We walked through the cold down the steep hill of Dickson Street, not saying much, and drifted into the early afternoon crowd at Roger's Pool Hall. This was after the *NY Times* write-up of the place. But the one thing Jim said that day to me that I can still recall wasn't profound, really, though I knew what he meant. We sat perched on those high metal stools at the bar, sipping the bourbon we both preferred, and he said "A man only loses his father once." It was okay to cry in Roger's, and I believe I did.

Jim had been gone nearly three years before I had the courage to call his widow, Gen Broyles, in Fayetteville and talk to her about the ideas I had for a book about Jim and his work. As gracious and warm as she always is, she invited me down to visit and see what was there. Part of what I found, I'm happy to say, has now become new books of his poetry: *The Panther* (Moon City Press) and *Common Need: New & Selected Poems* (University of Evansville Press). But at first I was overwhelmed by the boxes containing handwritten drafts on pad after yellow legal pad, and sometimes-typed manuscripts of two novels in progress.

What you have in *For, From, About James T. Whitehead* is both a *Gedenkschrift* and an offering. A book could have been made up of recollections and tributes alone. You'll read some very good ones here. You'll find impressive fiction, poetry, and creative nonfiction by teachers, graduates, and friends of the University of Arkansas Writing Program, among them a living President and an Inaugural Poet.

And I think you'll be delighted, as I was, to discover new fiction, poetry, and prose by Whitehead himself—just some of what we found waiting for us—first labored in love and anger and sweat across thousands of lines, imprinted by glasses and coffee cups, with running notes and commentary scrawled in the margins. I remember how carefully they were stacked into those boxes, as if he were thinking of someone like us.

James S. Baumlin

Textual Introduction and Acknowledgements

In his preface, Michael Burns writes of Whitehead's works "carefully . . . stacked into those boxes, as if he were thinking of someone like us." Whitehead had help, actually. In the summer of 2007, the author's widow, Gen Broyles, lent Whitehead's posthumous papers to the Missouri State University Library Special Collections and Archives. A graduate student in English, Craig A. Meyer spent the summer making an initial survey and reorganization of some 9.5 cubic feet of diverse archival materials (mostly drafts of unpublished novels, screenplays, and poems) that would become, officially, the James Tillotson Whitehead Collection. The graduate students in my fall 2007 research methods class—Judy Blackard, Judy Ermold, Charity Gibson, Jessica Glover, Leslie Hayes, Eric Knickerbocker, Kevin Luebbering, Mary Maupin, Ben Pfeiffer, Eric Sentell, Caleb Stokes, Cheng-Chun Tsai, Diana Tucker, and Sarah Viehmann—took on the collection as a team project, each contributing to the "finding aid" or descriptive inventory (100 pages total) that will accompany the collection when it comes to its final resting place, the Special Collections, University of Arkansas Libraries, Fayetteville.

What these students found will prove of abiding interest to Whitehead's colleagues and to scholars generally: multiple (though partial) drafts of *Bergeron* and *Coldstream*, both projected sequels to Whitehead's popular novel, *Joiner* (1971). Ever restless and experimenting in genre, Whitehead collaborated with his friend, B. C. Hall, over screenplay

3

versions of *Coldstream*, titled *Fair Game* and *The Fear Survey*, these provide an ending to the novel's otherwise unfinished plot. Whether or not the screenplays or novel-drafts are ever published, they are worth studying in tandem. So are the numerous poems remaining unpublished, many featuring the author's own scansion marks. Materials in the James Tillotson Whitehead Collection reveal the author's tortuous writing process, with draft after draft after draft of one and the same piece preserved side-by-side. Whitehead was an obsessive reviser, who would give a day's worrying to a single word or rhythm. Such care served him well when writing poetry, given the genre's linguistic concentration; when he wrote fiction, however, this same process led to near-paralysis— to hundreds (literally) of drafts, most starting from scratch, each subtly different from the rest, all drawing on the man's considerable poetic powers. Whitehead was always a poet, even when writing prose; given their uniqueness and inherently lyric quality, his longer drafts remain a delight to read—worth spending an afternoon in Special Collections.

I should say how this present volume came to be. In April 2008, the Creative Writing Program at the University of Arkansas, Fayetteville, marked its fortieth anniversary. In planning to celebrate the program that Whitehead helped found, Michael Burns (his former student) wrote to fellow alumni and to Whitehead's close friends, requesting contributions. Their outpouring of reminiscences and original works (in a variety of genres: short story, poetry, creative nonfiction) shows how admired and how influential Whitehead was among his fellow teachers, friends, and former students. Aided by several graduate students, Burns has edited and organized the collection into three major sections: hence the book's title, *For, From, and About* . . . . True, we have reordered the book's contents, putting "About Whitehead" first. But the poet would have forgiven us: put simply, *we liked the way the title sounded*, and did not want to sacrifice its euphony.

The first section, "About Whitehead," offers literary and personal remembrances from some of the man's most distinguished colleagues. Several are conscious imitations, playfully weaving allusions (to the man, his works, his haunts, even his habits of titling works) into the texts themselves. The second section, "From Whitehead," features original and hitherto unpublished works by Whitehead himself. (A fuller description of these follows.) The third section, "For Whitehead," is a gathering of works offered in tribute to the man, in several of the genres (and reflecting themes) he himself favored.

As several contributors attest, Whitehead was a lifelong devotee of visual art; serving as interchapters, we have included sets of photographs by Bruce West reflecting Whitehead's favorite stomping grounds, Mississippi (his childhood home and the subject of his writings) and the Ozarks. Taken together, the photographs present ironic contrasts between "wild" and "cultivated" nature—the "before" and "after" man culled it, cleared it, and prepared it for market. As a final treat, we present a brief family photo album interwoven with reminiscences from some of Whitehead's dearest friends. Framing the photo album are two quotations from Whitehead himself, both taken from his unpublished lecture, "The Bookworm, The Model Airplane, and The Spiritual Athlete." (We thank Kevin Luebbering for finding the lecture—it had been sandwiched in between notepad-drafts of *Bergeron*—and bringing it to our attention.)

Three graduate students who helped catalog the James Tillotson Whitehead Collection took on the task of selecting, transcribing, and partially text-editing the Whitehead materials printed posthumously here. A poet herself, Jessica Glover has made a careful selection from among the myriad drafts of poems. Of these, Whitehead's poem, "For Donald

5

Davidson," deserves an historical note. A segregationist and leading member of the Southern Agrarian movement, Davidson (1906–1968) was also an accomplished poet and critic who taught at Vanderbilt while Whitehead was a student there. In evaluating Davidson's writerly legacy, Whitehead's poem is at once commemorative and admonitory: "Read well before you turn his page," the poet cautions us.

Caleb Stokes transcribed and made an initial text-edit and abridgement of "Getting to Altamira," a piece of creative nonfiction whose curious history also deserves mention. In 1973 (following upon the success of *Joiner*), *OUI* magazine commissioned Whitehead to visit and write about Altamira. Brazil's military dictatorship had begun Trans-Amazonica, an ambitious public works project aimed at hacking a highway through the South American jungle. Springing up from the project, Altamira was rumored a rowdy frontier town— "violent and cunty," as Whitehead puts it—and of interest to the magazine's North American editors. After much procrastination, he produced a sixty-page narrative, sections of which are included here. Within the narrative, Whitehead writes about writing: "I'll do this right in fiction," he remarks to his fellow traveler, Dr. Bill Harrison. "This is an article," Dr. Bill replies.

The article was never published; neither was *Coldstream*, whose plot passes through the Amazon. Over three decades Whitehead returned time and again to this sequel novel, producing scores of partial drafts (most of them false starts and tinkerings) handwritten on yellow legal pads. A typescript survives, ending in mid-sentence on p. 269. Eric Sentell selected, transcribed, and edited an early manuscript version of the novel's opening chapter, which was published in *Moon City Review* 8:2 (2007), 13–21. Readers might compare this early version to the text presented here, which reprints the first two chapters of Whitehead's presumably "authoritative"

6

typescript. Here, too, we thank Mr. Sentell for assisting in evaluating and selecting text.

This project could not have borne fruit without the help and encouragement of many. First, of course, we thank Gen Broyles for allowing us access to Whitehead's posthumous papers and for granting permission to publish them, along with family photographs. We thank David Richards, Anne Baker, and Tracie Gieselman-Holthaus of the Missouri State University Library Special Collections and Archives: providing temporary shelter for Whitehead's papers, they offered all resources at their disposal, turning Special Collections into a classroom for the graduate students who read and inventoried each page. And we thank the editors at University of Evansville Press for sharing two of Whitehead's posthumous poems with us. "Mistress of Vines and Earthen Crocks: For Gen" and "Lecture" will be published concurrently here and in their forthcoming Whitehead collection, *Common Need: New & Selected Poems*. (We hope that our readers will buy their book, and *vice versa*).

First planned as an April 2008 publication, our little book proved longer in the making than anticipated. Hence, we need to thank the editors of *No Magazine* (2008) for sharing four poems from C. D. Wright's collection, *40 Watts*. Our excerpt was supposed to beat them to press; they in fact beat us. Similarly, we thank the editors at Louisiana State University Press for permission to reprint Miller Williams's "The Alphabet as Part of What We Do and Are" and "An Unrhymed Sonnet," both of which have appeared in *Time and the Tilting Earth* (2008). The same holds for Beth Ann Fennelly's "The Welcoming: an *Ars Poetica*," which has appeared in *Unmentionables: Poems* (2008). "Telling the Gospel Truth" first appeared in her collection, *Tender Hooks* (2004). Given its "Whiteheadesque" themes (on living, loving, and the teaching of poetry), we are pleased to include an excerpt from this larger work. We thank W. W. Norton for permission

7

to reprint both of Fennelly's poems. Dave Smith's "Red Dress" revises a poem that first appeared in the journal, *Five Points* (2008), published by Georgia State University. Charles d'Orléans' *Ballade* (ably translated by John Duval) is quoted from *Poesies*, ed. Pierre Champion (Paris: Librairie Ancienne, 1923).

Leon Stokesbury has incorporated a poem, "To Laura Phelan: 1880–1906," into his larger prose remembrance of Whitehead. This and two other lyrics, "The Lover Remembereth As He Sometimes Enjoyed and Showeth How He Would Like To Enjoy Her Again," and "To All Those Considering Coming to Fayetteville," are reprinted from Stokesbury's *Autumn Rhythm* (1996). We thank the University of Arkansas Press for permission to reprint these gems about living and lusting (and drinking) in Fayetteville during "the age of Whitehead." In similar manner, Jo McDougall tells the story behind "For Stephen, Who Owns a Bag of My Cut Fingernails Carried in the Mouth of an Eel Who Swam the Caddo." First published in *Dirt* (2001), the poem (in both its title and length) shows Whitehead's looming influence. We thank the press editors at Autumn House for permission to reprint it. Excerpted here, Steve Yates's "Coin of the Realm" first appeared in the journal, *Valley Voices* (2008). As suggested by Yates's subtitle ("Or: A Local Student Recognizes How Jim Whitehead Can Inhabit Any Character Who Is Large and Radiates Mysterious Force"), Whitehead's presence abides in the theme and, indeed, characterization. The "outhouse meditation" narrated in W. D. Blackmon's "Ruby" is taken from a larger piece, first published in *Midwestern Humanities Review* (1999).

We have further debts. Angelia Northrip-Rivera, a senior instructor in the English department at Missouri State University, provided the text layout. Rebecca Sloane of Missouri State University Printing Services designed the cover. Dr. Tita F. Baumlin, our colleague in English, helped type and proof the manuscript. Tom Lavoie of the University of Arkansas Press gave his typically sage advice throughout the various stages of book production. Barbara Gressel, head secretary of the Missouri State University English department, served (as always) as the heavenly Muse of Moon City Press.

JAMES T. WHITEHEAD

A Dedication
Mistress of Vines and Earthen Crocks: For Gen

Mistress of vines and earthen crocks, she makes
This house a jungle living off our breath—
Lean fronds emerge from every corner. Stakes
Outside hold up the trees she planted. Wrath

Attacks the April snow. She prays for rain
And bears another human child. I write
Long novels describing how green is pain—
She gets ripe again, scents the night

And touches on my abstract thumb. What name?
Thank God she asks me for their names, a plant
In Latin is my hope, a Norwegian boy
Is chosen out of all the dead. I can't

Compete with nature. She is perfect joy
Against the dying of this sorry world.
Bless us, dear God, when we are barely old.

Jim and Gen Whitehead, 1966

Jim and Gen Whitehead, 1995
(Courtesy of Gen Broyles)

About Whitehead

"Soon After I Returned Home To Plains": A Letter

Soon after I returned home to Plains from the White House in 1981, Jim Whitehead and Miller Williams came to give a poetry reading in our town. This unprecedented literary event was held in the restaurant operated by Sybil Carter, the widow of my brother Billy. A good portion of our local citizens turned out for the readings, and during an interlude I mentioned that I had written a poem or two myself, but didn't know anything about rhyme, meter, syntax, or the proper choice of words.

Perhaps seduced by the culinary beauty of the barbecued ribs and sweet potato pie, the two professors offered to take me on as a long-distance student, and I accepted their proposal. The two basic commitments were that I would accept their imposition of strict discipline and unrestrained criticism and they would not suggest a particular word in any of my lines. This struggle lasted for more than a dozen years, and a book of my poems was finally published.

I enjoyed meeting with Jim and Miller on occasion, either in Plains, Fayetteville, or at a place about halfway between the two, so we could have some face-to-face instruction in addition to relying on the postal service. I recall that Jim especially concentrated on a haiku about Mount Fuji and the only sonnet I wrote, entitled "Plains."

I have relished Jim's poetry and consider *Joiner* to be one of the South's best novels. He meant a lot to me, and I'm grateful for his friendship.

BETH ANN FENNELLY

Remembering Jim Whitehead, Teacher and Friend

In the autumn of 1995, Tom Franklin and I were newly-smitten grad students at the University of Arkansas, and we moved in together, finding a rental house on Lindell Avenue for $450 dollars a month. The house was small, square, beige, and cheaply built; it was so close to the stadium that we could hear the marching band and feel the rumble through the floorboards when the Razorbacks scored.

When Christmas neared that first year, I hung an evergreen wreath on the front door, and after Christmas break Tommy and I returned to Fayetteville to find our little house had squatters—that is, a pair of house finches had built their nest in the wreath. A few days later, in the tree by our front door, I found another nest had been built by a pair of robins. The weeks got warmer and Tommy and I counted three blue robin eggs in the tree nest and four brown freckled finch eggs in the door nest. They hatched within a few days of each other, and we had seven cheeping frizzy-headed birds, a hatchling sub-division. I liked to walk home from Kimpel and stand between the two nests, wait quietly enough that the Mamas didn't mind me and left to fetch some food, then returned with squirming worms that they'd drop down the yearning, upturned beaks. One day while I stood there, I saw something surprising. As the mama robin returned with a worm for her babies, she flew past the nest on the front door, and one hungry finch was straining so desperately and cheeping so loudly that she dropped the worm right down his throat instead of giving it to her own young.

16

An ornithologist pal later confirmed what I saw. Animals sometimes will feed the young of another species. The urge to feed is a strong urge, he told me, and it can be very hard to resist an open mouth.

Tommy and I moved from that cheap plywood house nearly seven years ago. So, now, why do I return to it again and again and again to open that door? Because I miss Jim Whitehead, the man and the teacher. When people talk about the uncontrollable human urges, they usually mean jealousy or hate. But there are others, and I think for Jim, the desire to educate was an uncontrollable urge. He could no better stand to let an ignorant, poetry-hungry student go unfed than that mama robin could stand to see the yawping beak of a hungry bird when she had something to give.

The first time I realized how deeply the impulse to educate coursed through Jim was when Tommy and I scraped up enough frequent flyer miles to go to Paris for spring break. Jim and his colleague, Skip Hayes, were on the continent too and when we discovered we'd all be in Paris at the same time, we made plans to meet at the Musée D'Orsay. When Tommy and I arrived, Jim and Skip seemed glad to see us. Soon they were shepherding us from painting to painting, communicating their enthusiasms. Jim would place us before Chagall's great "The Circus," point out its animal symbolism, and tell us about Chagall's life and his long and loving marriage to his wife. Then Skip showed us a Manet and traced for us the influence of the Japanese print-making which was admired by the French impressionists. Then Jim corralled us towards a Picasso. Jim and Skip gave a better, more impassioned tour than any official, expensive guide, I'm sure. Far from the classrooms of Fayetteville, these two men still felt moved to share the considered and beautiful ways they'd learned to view the world. We knew we were lucky to have them to teach us. Later I realized they too were lucky that we were there to be taught, for great teachers are happiest when teaching, and without us, they might have just interrupted each other all afternoon, eventually growing frustrated when they couldn't top each other. I remember that day and the long evening that followed—an evening of drinking wine on the banks of the Seine while the sun set and across the flashing water an unseen drummer beat his bongos and we shared confidences—as being one of the finest times of my life.

Whether in the museums of Paris or the halls of Kimpel where he tortured—oops, I mean tailored—comp exams to each student's history and learning, Jim had the soul of a teacher. He taught us constantly, relentlessly, desperately. He taught us courtesy stress, and courtesy, and stress, he called us by our last names, as if he were our coach, and, of course, he was, he said more with his devilish eyebrows than some people say in whole paragraphs, in workshop he could be dead-on accurate or completely miss the point, in his commentary he was sometimes cryptic and quixotic, in his sensitivities he was both winning and exasperating, and we grin, don't we, as we remember how he shouted once in workshop, "I am not touchy." An intellectual omnivore, he studied WWI, Hank Williams, Simone Weil, the beaches of Normandy, the life of Christ, the poems of Bishop, fundraising, the law, every good person in the State of Mississippi, the pet peeves of administrators. He studied life like he could be tested on any subject at any time and he wanted to get an A plus. It's impossible to imagine someone asking Jim a question and him answering, "Sorry, that's not my field." I worked with him as the program assistant and when I picture him in his office I picture him leaning back precariously in his straining office chair, mulling over some problem with the program or WITS or fundraising, and then hitting upon a solution, lunging forward to grab the phone, pulling it towards him with one hand and settling his glasses on his nose with the other, so he could concentrate as he

18

mashed the tiny number buttons with his giant blunt-tipped fingers.

I keep the notes from his Form and Theory of Poetry class on my writing desk—that's how good they are. Not as near at hand but perhaps even more important were the lessons he gave us outside of class, at his patio table with a handful of students arguing poetry and trading jokes over bowls of dry-roasted peanuts and Snyder's Hard pretzels as the night came on and the cicadas laid their bass line. Nights like these, I'd wander inside to find Gen making tea and ask her advice about my struggles with Catholicism and receive her practical, revolutionary answers, then, after a while, help myself to another beer and return to the dark summer stew of lightning bugs and my classmates' laughter and Jim's big voice and its various challenges and now perhaps another professor such as Brian Wilke or Skip would have joined the group and the stories would rise and settle, rise and settle like waves.

I still can't believe I'll never see his big red face again. But I know Jim is more present in death than most people ever are in life. All those ways he had of feeding us—"Fennelly, have you read Milton?" he'd demand; "You of all people need Milton," and he of course was right—all those ways he fed us have become part of us, embodied and alive in us. Here, an excerpt from my Form and Theory notes on Yeats' great sonnet, "Leda and the Swan": "Does she take on his knowledge with his power?" Jim questioned, "What does a human learn from passionate experience? What do we take with us from a painful event that leaves us forever changed?" What indeed did we learn in the passionate experiences of being Jim's students? What do we take from the painful event of his death? He gave himself to us, and if we went on to become writers, he writes through us. Through our hands, his giant fingers grip their yellow number two pencil across the yellow legal pad. And if we went on to become teachers,

19

his example challenges us to give ourselves more generously to *our* students. Through our voices, his massive knowledge rehearses and enlarges itself, and is jotted down in the notebooks of our students, students he's never met but are the better because he lived, because for 67 glorious years Jim Whitehead fed us, fed us, fed us every time he could.

Jim Whitehead at Vanderbilt

I was a graduate student—sophisticated, I thought—cruising between classes in literature, philosophy, and theology, and writing a bit of poetry and short fiction. As an undergraduate back in Texas I had edited the campus newspaper and hung out with the cynics—including veterans of the Korean War. I had read the Russian novelists and James Joyce. I looked down on piety and pretense. At Vanderbilt I had a considerably more intellectual environment than I had known in Texas and I intended to study and teach comparative religion but novels and the theater kept getting in the way. I was directing a play at a local playhouse, Arthur Miller's *A View From the Bridge*.

The hot philosophy professor that semester in 1958 was teaching a course in existentialism and I threw the word around with everybody else although nobody knew exactly what it meant. There was Sartre on one side and Kierkegaard on the other. Confusing, and no one could define it exactly. Phillip Hallie, our instructor, was back from a Guggenheim year, a cockbird like the rest of us, young, erudite, and pacing back and forth in an elongated room—three long rows of desk chairs that allowed him thirty feet to wave his hands before us—in a frenzy of language and insight.

Then Jim Whitehead roared into the room.

It was the second or third class. He was late enrolling.

He entered as Hallie lectured, yanked a desk chair out of the front row down at the far end of the room, tried to fit himself into it, dropped his books, excused himself loudly, then as Hallie tried to recover his train of thought Jim began to talk. He barked out questions and assertions. He wrestled with his desk chair. He was six-foot-five inches tall and weighed 240 pounds. He had been recruited to play offensive tackle on the football team, but a shoulder injury had waylaid him so he had taken up art and literature with raw intensity.

From that moment the existentialism class—intellectual chaos, at best—was somehow taught by a gifted young philosophy professor and this undergraduate giant.

Whitehead came late every day, smacking his desk chair around, having read the assignment, on the attack. He was a disruption, a comedy act, a force field. Hallie liked him. Jim was existentialism itself. The classroom walls fell down.

Some weeks into the course I introduced myself.

"I'm directing this play by Arthur Miller," I said, looking up at him. "The lead character is a big longshoreman named Eddie Carbone. The leader of a huge, unruly family. I'd like you to play the part. No audition. Just come play the part."

Jim, pulling himself up and becoming even larger, became Eddie Carbone before my eyes and agreed.

During the rehearsals and the run of the play we became friends. His girlfriend, Gen, and my young wife, Merlee, became lifelong friends too. He introduced me to his pals at the apartment house on Capers Avenue—including young John Yount who became my friend and fishing buddy. (Yount and I took Phil Hallie on a fishing trip and drank approximately a pint of Hennessey's brandy for every trout we landed.)

Jim was a magnificent actor—and remained so all his life. Since we played in a theater-in-the-round my task was to keep him moving so that the other actors could be seen. He smoked cigars and everyone choked on the smoke. He mesmerized the audience and once dropped a large portion of ash onto a woman's skirt during a gesture. She gazed up at his contorted face and never noticed.

We all confessed that we wanted to be writers. We published our stories and poems in *The Vagabond*, the literary magazine at Vanderbilt. Jim was writing a long and outlandish novel set in Mississippi called *The Growth* in which kudzu was a major symbolism. Yount's wife, Susie, joined the circle of friends. We stayed up far past every midnight talking: literature and life, the great agonies of the young, beautiful and serious. I taught our two-year-old daughter, Laurie, to master the words "Boris Pasternak is a Russian writer" and everyone appropriately fell back and laughed when she gave them the line. The men drank too much. The years ahead were dark promises.

By 1964 I was at the University of Arkansas where it was agreed that I'd start an MFA program in fiction and poetry. We needed a poet and Jim was at Millsaps College and had published his first book of verse. I wanted a big guy, a manly poet, not some wistful little suck up, and with a phone call to make there was only one man to call.

He changed not much from that time he slammed through the door and into the classroom: a brave intellect, seldom in doubt, theatrical, generous.

LEON STOKESBURY

In Another Country

When I came to the MFA program at the University of Arkansas in 1968, I experienced something a bit like culture shock. Not that Fayetteville was a thriving urban or urbane center back then, but in those days if you were from the country, as I was, you really *were* from the country. I had grown up about seven or eight miles outside of a very small East Texas town in a world before internet or cable TV or DVDs or multiplexes or even malls. Just folks. And some books. And my undergraduate career had been spent carpooling from my parents' home, about thirty-five miles, five days a week, to the nearest seat of higher learning, The Lamar State College of Technology, in Beaumont.

When I arrived in Fayetteville, about all I had going for me was a truly obsessive love for the reading and writing of poetry. And as luck would have it, I happened to arrive at a place where the professor with whom I would study most closely for the next several years happened to have a deep, maybe even obsessive, love for teaching the reading and writing of poetry. Over those years, Jim Whitehead and I managed to work out a fairly strong symbiotic relationship, and finally a friendship, based on these mutual obsessions.

But that is not to say things always went smoothly. There were a number of times in the late sixties and early seventies when my defensive student attempts to define myself as what I conceived to be a "poet" in the "ever-changing world of today," et cetera, got me into quite ridiculous and sometimes even illegal situations. A few of these I managed to extricate myself from on my own, and a few others required Jim

Whitehead's assistance, and then there was one or two that, I must admit, were actually perpetrated on that major professor. When I think back to those days, quite fondly I confess, I am more thankful than I was ever able to say for Jim's patience and, I can see now, his understanding.

Which brings me to my point. One incident in particular always comes to mind first when I do my remembering. The reason for this is that there was this one "graduate student prank" that, eventually, did end up resulting in something positive.

In May of 1969, the last week of my first spring semester in the MFA program, I remember that the poem I had on the worksheet that week was not well received. I do not now remember which poem of mine it was, just that Jim and the rest of the class had made it clear that they felt I had not been visited by any muse during its construction. This was not the first time this had happened, most certainly, but I do remember that it bothered me particularly. And I think it may have been partially behind some of my actions the next Saturday night. I, and a number of other poets in the program, often spent Friday and/or Saturday night at one or two of the bars on Dickson Street. The ones we frequented most often were aptly called *The Swinging Door* and the ineptly named *George's Majestic Lounge*. Anyway, after spending several hours in these places, and then spending another couple of hours after closing time continuing to drink beer in, as I recall, my apartment, everyone went home to sleep except me and one other poet named Paul Lubenkov. We decided to keep going. And it was then that I got the idea to put a tombstone in Jim Whitehead's front yard. There was a very old, filled-up graveyard on Dickson Street, just off campus, and we were both sure that we could find exactly what we needed there. And we did. It was not easy. By three o'clock in the morning, we were, alas, not thinking too clearly.

So, we drove to the cemetery. We lowered the chain across the road and drove, in the dark, into the middle of this place. To those who have never tried to do such a thing, one of the immediate problems is the weight of the stone. Even small tombstones are very heavy, and awkward. But we did find one that was a little over two feet high with a solid base. We loaded it into the trunk of my car, well over a hundred and fifty pounds, and then drove to Jim's house on Lafayette Street. Then we backed the car up into his yard, and somehow we managed to get the thing out of the trunk and set up in the middle of his front lawn. Ha. Ha.

Around nine the next morning, I was awakened by the phone ringing. Amazedly, Jim had deduced that I was the one who would have done such a thing. He did not even ask if I were the guilty party. He said he wanted me to come over right now and get it off his lawn. It was Mother's Day, and his wife was not amused. I actually think Jim did not mind the whole thing very much, but it was evidently proving a tad harder for Gen to share in the levity. Usually, she suffered us gladly. That day she wasn't interested in suffering us at all.

I called Paul Lubenkov and we went to the Whiteheads' and then took the stone back to the cemetery. We figured that no one would mind our taking something *back*. And no one was there to mind, but unfortunately in the daylight we could not find the place where we had gotten the stone the night before. Everything seemed completely different. After looking for fifteen minutes or so, we found what looked like an empty plot and set the stone there as if it belonged, and then we got the hell out.

Well, that much is true. And it has little significance, even to me, except for what happened about a year later. One night I could not sleep. I recognized how I felt as that often longed-for but seldom-felt psychic itch that meant I was about ready to write something. About, dare I suggest it, to be visited by the muse. And the tombstone incident came into my head. I got up and wrote a poem imagining going back to the tombstone and asking questions of it. Big questions. I did rearrange and stretch a few of the facts, for artistic purposes. But it is true that I never did find out where the actual grave was. And that is also what the poem is about. The woman, or anyone, as far as the living are concerned, had become this rock with her name on it, this artifact.

Of all the poems I wrote while in the Arkansas MFA program, that one, "To Laura Phelan: 1880–1906," is the one I can read today with the least amount of teeth grinding. And it came about, I can see now, in large part because of James Whitehead's patience, and his ability to suffer me somewhat gladly, mostly.

To Laura Phelan: 1880–1906

Drunk I have been. And drunk I was that night
I lugged your stone across the other graves,
to set you up a hundred yards away.
Flowers I found, then. Drunk I have been.
And am, standing here with no moon to spill
on the letters of your name; my loud fingers
feeling them out. The stone is mossed over.
And why must I bring myself in the dark
to stand here among the sour grasses
that stain my white jeans? Drunk I have been.
See, the thick dew slides on the trees, wet weeds,
wetness smears the air; and a vague surf
of wildflowers pushes my feet, slipping
close to my legs. When the thought comes at last
that people fall apart, that the things we do
will not do. Ends. Then, we come to scenes
like this. This scene of you. You apart:

this is not you; and yet, this is where I stand
and close my eyes, and feel the ragged wind
blow red and maul my hair. In the night somewhere,
dandelions foam. This is not you. Drunk
I have been. Across this graveyard, that
is where you are. Yet I stand here. Would ask
things of your name. Would wish. Would not be told
of the stink in the skull, the eye's collapse.
Would be told something new, something unknown.—
A mosquito bites my hand. The only sound
is the rough wind. Drunk I have been,
here, at the loam's maw, before this stone
of yours, which is not you. Which is.

JOHN DUFRESNE

Bricoleur

The two of you were in his study discussing the line from "This Be the Verse" about your mum and dad, how they fuck you up. This was years ago in Fayetteville. He said, "Dufresne, how can you expect to understand Philip Larkin if you haven't read Schopenhauer?" And then he called the Dickson Street Bookshop and told them to hold a copy of The World As Will and Representation *and sent you off to buy it. He said, "We'll talk when you've finished reading it." On the poster taped to the ceiling above your heads, Vermeer's* Girl with a Pearl Earring *shimmered with light. She looked like she was waiting for you, or waiting for you to say something.*

When your father said, "How could you do this to me?" and dropped the little magazine with your short story in it on the coffee table, you said, "Yes, Dad, the narrator's father has only one arm just like you, and, yes, he's a greeter at Wal-Mart just like you, but he's not you. I made him up. His name's Jake, yours is Jack. His hair's a shade lighter than yours. It's fiction, Dad."

Your father wasn't buying it. "You think I dress like a rodeo clown?"

"Not you. Jake."

And then he recited the line where Jake tells his son he's dead to him. "I never said that, dammit." And, of course he did, and you both know it. So now your family's off limits. You can't even use your cousin Babbo, at least not until his mother, your aunt Claudie dies. She's your favorite, and she'd be hurt. (And to be honest, Babbo's a little hard to believe anyway.) "From now on, don't trifle with people's lives," your father said. "Make up your goddamn characters. You got an imagination. Use it!"

Fuck you, Dad. (You think it; you don't say it.)

So now you'd like to write a story, and you even have an idea for one, a story of fatal imprudence, wherein curiosity (of the amorous variety) results in the "loss of the possession of a loved one." (You've been reading George Polti's *The Thirty-Six Dramatic Situations* and this is Situation Seventeen B [2].) Or maybe you'll just steal a plot. Why not? A person sets off on a quest. A stranger rides into town. How hard can it be? But first you need to assemble a character. So you take an articulate gesture from the person who sat across from you on the bus, a turn of phrase overheard at the Laundromat, one woman's statuesque posture, a gentleman's limp (and you think, yes, every scar tells a story, doesn't it?, and you make a note in your Evidence memo pad), an engaging smile here, a curious tic there, and you build a character around the details. You take a hairstyle from this one, a breathy voice from that one, a remarkable event from one guy's life, a childhood trauma from another's.

(You learned about said remarkable—and grisly—event [the narrator's brother was scalded with boiling water, and the burned skin eventually slipped off the brother's fingers like an oiled chicken-skin glove, and so on] while you were having lunch at the Japanese place on the boulevard [crispy bok choy and yakiniku steak] and you were eavesdropping on the hushed exchange coming from the booth behind you and writing it all down on a napkin with the pen you borrowed from the waitress—yes, what about that waitress! She [the name tag said "Cosette"] sat across from you when she took your order, said she had to rest her aching feet [her "tired puppies" was how she put it], asked what you were reading, and when you showed her the cover of *The World As Will and Representation*, she rolled her eyes and asked you if you really had time for pessimism, and you wondered whom she goes home to after her shift and what she finds there and what she doesn't, and you realized you'd discovered another character, this one as fully assembled as an ex-wife. "White or brown rice?" she said. "White." "Saki?" "Sapporo." She wasn't wearing make-up as far as you could tell. She *was* wearing a man's white oxford shirt, a black skirt, black ankle socks and white running shoes. She had these smile lines on her right cheek. Dark eyes. And she wore a blue and white striped silk tie, loose at the collar. She said, "No spicy Manila clams tonight?" You said, "Do you know me?" "I know your type," she said.)

Later that night you find yourself outside Cosette's house. You knock. She opens the door and says, "I can't say this is unexpected." You smile and hand her the borrowed pen and the gift. You tell her it's a Kindle, something new. It holds two hundred books, and you lie to her and say you've downloaded the Modern Library's 100 Best Novels and 100 Best Nonfiction books of the twentieth century for her. Actually you downloaded your own books. And Larkin and some Schopenhauer and Chekhov. Who could afford two hundred? You sit on the sofa, and she settles into a rocking chair with the Kindle in her lap. She's wearing jeans rolled to her calves to show off her two Japanese ankle tattoos. One is a winged, fire-breathing dragon, the other, in Japanese characters, is a quote from Sei Shonagon, "All small things are adorable." Why did you lie to her?

"All of our sorrows spring out of our relations to other people," you say.

She tells you she has found the opposite to be true.

You tell her something can be true and untrue at the same time.

Her black T-shirt says this in white typescript: "Most things will never happen. This one will."

You admire Cosette's living room while she goes to the kitchen to mix two martinis. There's a white enamel colander filled with sea shells on an end table and a spray of violets in a glass pitcher. She has an herb garden growing in an old wooden beer crate by the bay window. On the wall beside the kitchen door there's a tarnished silver spoon mounted on white cardboard and framed. On the wall opposite are a mirror draped in black cloth and a large tin milagro of a flaming heart. When she returns, you tell her how clever you think she is. "My little projects," she says. "I use whatever's lying around." She hands you your drink. "Here's to making do," she says. "To a life without irony."

"And what's this?" You mean the wooden box with a collection of metal film canisters under glass.

"Making art," she says.

"It's art because . . . ?"

"Because we don't need it." She sips her drink. "Too much vermouth?"

"Mine's perfect."

"Don't need it in order to survive, I mean. But we can't really live without it."

In your dream the two of you are walking in front of Old Main, and when you tell him about the trouble you're having with your narrative, he tells you you're doing it all wrong. "It doesn't breathe," he says. "Story! Story! Story! Goddamnit," he says. "What do I do?" you say. He says, "Bring in a cousin from Illinois." He sucks on his True Blue, exhales the smoke out the side of his mouth, and waves it away from his eyes. "Even better, have a man with a gun walk through the door. Something's bound to happen. Have him burst through the fucking door waving a .38 Ruger in front of his face. Let him fire a shot through the empty Morris chair." "You think?" you say. "And suddenly the story deepens like a coastal shelf," he says.

32

You tell Cosette you're thinking of stealing a plot for her.

"My life isn't interesting enough?"

"Life doesn't come with plots."

"Except the one they bury you in."

"Beginning, muddle, and end."

"So you're a thief," she says. "Well, I'm all finished with bad boys."

You tell her you're writing a story. She says she's worth a novel. You tell her you don't have a novel in you right now. "And I'm not a bad boy. I write. I don't even have a life."

Someone kicks the door in, and before you can turn, a shot rings out, and a bullet tears through the green cushion on the Morris chair. What you notice is the fluff from the wounded chair floating in the wake of the shot. You squeeze your eyes shut. Your ears are ringing.

Cosette says, "Goddamnit, Babbo, you're going to kill someone."

"You know Babbo?" you say.

"He comes by now and then," she says.

You turn to him. He smiles and tips his hat. You say, "Babbo, I'm afraid I'm going to have to ask you to leave."

Later, Cosette tells you that Babbo enjoys dressing in women's clothing.

"My Babbo?" you say. You knew about his appetite for euphoriants, his fear of milk, and his compulsive lying. You knew about the abduction by Satanists, his second self, and the abandoned wife and children. You didn't know about his uncommon fashion sense.

"He says it makes his heart beat faster."

"I can't use him," you tell her, and you mention your father's anger and your aunt's tender feelings.

"Every writer's family is doomed," she says.

"Babbo's full of surprises."

33

You tell her that when Babbo graduated from the Moody Bible Institute, he took a preaching job in New Hampshire and married an affable and selfless young woman in his congregation. They had the twin boys, Perez and Zerah, the restored eighteenth-century farmhouse, the clerical and civic duties, and then Babbo disappeared. He turned up a year later in St. Louis. He said he was committed to a mental hospital. He told the doctors he was Harris Chapman, from Cambridge, Ohio, but when they gave him some truth serum, he suddenly remembered it all, how he'd been abducted that night by Satanists and had been strapped down in the back of a GMC Vandura that smelled like lamb and had had his brain washed with an electric machine attached to his forehead that made him forget his life as a minister, forget his wife and family, forget himself. He didn't know why they turned him into a Harris Chapman, however, or why they gave him a Harris Chapman's memories.

"Poor Babbo," Cosette says.

"He and his reunited family lived in Harmony, New York, for several years before he vanished again, this time for fifteen years. When a nephew eventually tracked him down, Babbo was the Honorable Harris Chapman II, mayor of Teapot Hollow, Tennessee. The gig was up. He came back home. He told me he left his family the second time because the very same Satanic cult had given him a choice—"to see my family slaughtered in front of my eyes or to go with them. I chose to run. There'd be bodies in graves right now, Johnny.""

Cosette says, "You're making this up."

"True story. No word of a lie."

"Did he get back with his wife?"

"She'd had him declared dead after seven years and remarried a stump grinder in Harmony. Doing real well, I'm told."

"So Babbo's legally dead?"

"But living with his mother."

"Poor woman."

"She's happy to have him. Says he was always an excitable boy."

"But you can't write about him."

"But I can write about you."

Cosette tells you that at twenty-two she was engaged to a man she met at college, a doctor. She loved Felix to death. But when she got pregnant, he suggested that starting a family just then might be bad timing what with his residency and their debts, so she had the child aborted. Had the pregnancy terminated, she says. And still she has to stop herself from thinking about what might have been, from imagining her son—she just knows it was a boy—now at eighteen. "Our love did not survive the loss."

She tells you how she then immersed herself in her career, and in her domestic and civic responsibilities (the Rotary Cub, the Lions Club, the Young Democrats). She was a staff pharmacist for one of the big drug-store chains. She simply had no time to conduct a whirlwind romance. Pretty soon the only guys hitting on her were the happily married Rotarians. "Then my girlfriend Cindy told me there was nothing wrong with Internet dating. And, to be honest, I was tired of eating alone at restaurants. Cindy told me they screen the wackos right out.

"Not all the wackos, apparently," she says. Cosette wound up dating Robert the technical-support consultant with the curious Belgian accent who never seemed to have a steady job and who blushed at first when he asked to borrow money from her, but got over his timidity soon enough. Then the marathon runner who couldn't stop looking at himself in shop windows and who built his life around competitions and wouldn't have sex before a race so as not to sap his vital bodily fluids. And Marvin the Lexus salesman (he tried to sell her a pre-owned LS) and Civil War reenactor, who bought her a promenade dress with pagoda sleeves and a hooped skirt and asked her to wear it around the house. "I decided eating alone wasn't so bad," she says.

"I always take a book with me," you say.

She holds up her Kindle and smiles. "I met Dario at the blackjack table at the Hard Rock. I was with Cindy. She made herself scarce." Cosette was Dario's lucky charm, he told her. He bought her a dinner at Tequila Ranch. One thing led to another, and all the dark comedy of the computer dates gave way to the breathless elation of romance. "This was three years ago. It was easier to fall in love than I'd remembered." Dario was considerate, witty, attentive, and affectionate. He had two boys, Caden and Cole, seven-year-olds, from a former (well, not quite former) wife. He had the boys every other weekend and seemed devoted to them. In fact, he told Cosette that she had to understand that his kids came first in his life, a sentiment she both admired and resented.

"But the course of true love never does run smooth. You know that," she says.

"I depend on it," you say.

She tells you that Dario hesitated in getting the divorce. This despite his protestations of love. She told herself how frightened he must be thinking he might hurt his boys, might lose their love, their respect. She was disappointed when he went through with a planned fishing trip with his pals on her birthday. There'll be other birthdays, he told her, and he kissed her forehead. She was in love and would not permit these disappointments and frustrations to get in the way. She pursued Dario with all the grace and passion she had. She allowed herself to be unguarded and susceptible. It's how you have to be when you've found *the one*. Dario was a sales supervisor at Best Buy. He had his eye on a district manager's slot.

"So this one weekend when the boys joined me and Dario at my place, Cole came down with a stomach virus. I called Phyllis, the mom, by then Dario's ex, and let her know Cole's situation. 'He's up watching TV and eating chicken soup.' Phyllis told me she'd buy me a drink when Dario eventually, inevitably dumped me.

"'Oh, I know he's not perfect,' I said.

"'He's not even who you think he is.'

"'He's so sweet to me.'

"'Where is he now?'

"'At his rent house doing some minor repairs.'

"'You probably don't want to drop by unannounced.'"

Meanwhile there were other difficulties in her life, Cosette tells you. ("And this is where it becomes a novel. So you can just skip what you don't need.") Her beloved dad took ill, and her mom fell to pieces with worry. The pharmacy chain was closing the local store and wanted her to transfer to a Midwest location. There was a sizeable raise included. Dario, of course, couldn't leave the area, what with the boys and all. At the hospital, Cosette's dad had expressed some doubts about Dario. Call it a hunch. "Why isn't he here with you now?" her dad asked her.

She and Dario had their most serious disagreement over children. He didn't want another one. She desperately wanted a child, and her time to conceive was running out. Nothing was settled, but Cosette figured she could make a pregnancy happen through guile or charm, and now was not the time for unnecessary honesty. Dario stopped by the Hard Rock some days after work, but he didn't like going with her anymore. And didn't like her going on her own. It didn't look right, that's all. He could be pretentious and had turned off her friends with all his pontificating about wine and cheese. He fancied himself a political moderate, but he sounded a lot like a typically rabid conservative with his hostility toward immigrants and the impoverished. Where did all that anger come from? Or was it fear? Some days Cosette wondered if this struggle wasn't all too much. She felt like her own life was on hold sometimes. But then she would remember that night.

"We were snowbound in a cabin in Vermont. No power, no phone service. The drafty windows rattled in the wind. So we snuggled by the fire, sipped brandy, and talked into the night." He told her about his childhood, about his dad's abandonment of the family, something he never really got over, how he missed his dad and hated him at the same time. He told her how as a boy he had dreamed of becoming a pilot, but being a sales supervisor wasn't such a bad life. He told her about his new dream, and he sat up and stared into the fire when he did, like he was almost afraid to look at her when he spoke. He saw himself—"I mean the two of us"—on an island off the coast of Maine living a simple and resolute life. "We're self-sufficient. We learn to read the land and the sea. Maybe we buy a lobster boat. We're together, and we have very little, but we're rich in love." She put her head on his arm and told him they could make that happen. And they made love by the fire, and he did not turn away when they had finished. She watched him sleep until the sun came up, and she got up and relit the fire and looked out on the land draped in snow as smooth as a baby's talced bottom, and even the fir trees, iced in cake frosting, seemed to share her happiness. The memory and promise of that night were reason enough for her to overlook the little annoyances.

And so she took the severance offer from the firm and decided to worry about her next real job after the wedding. Maybe start her own business. In the meantime she'd waitress on weekdays. And she busied herself with plans for the honeymoon. And so on. And then she looks at you and says, "You know how it feels on your skin when a cloud passes before the sun? Well, that's how I felt when I saw him walk into the restaurant. I knew what he was going to say before he said it."

"He told you at work that it was over? What a shit."

"That was five months ago. Knocked me for a loop. And suddenly it all made sense, the supposedly vacant rent house, his stops at the casino, the lipstick case I found in his car that he said was the ex-wife's—it had all been a lie." She claps her hands together three times as if she's wiping them clean, and says, "End . . . of . . . story!"

"All our sorrows . . ." you say.

"Spring from our ignorance. Our willful ignorance."

"True and untrue."

"Why couldn't I see what was so obvious?"

"They say our eyes clear with age."

Jim's gone now, but he's still talking, and he tells you to listen to Cosette. "That woman understands you need to go to where you got the wound. You write from where you got the wound. You open yourself to suffering. You're damn lucky she found you, son." You tell him you found her. He shakes his head and says, "What you don't know would make a good goddamn book." You have to agree. "A big book," you say. He grabs onto your shoulder and squeezes. "Well, it's what you don't know that's important."

She says, "Let me freshen that drink for you." She gets up. She says, "Phyllis owes me a drink, come to think of it."

"You're better off, you know, without the bastard."

"I live alone," she says. When she gets to the kitchen door she stops, turns, and stares back at you, and the light catches the diamond in her ear. It looks like she's waiting for you, or waiting for you to write something.

The last thing Jim says is, "Don't fuck this up!"

For Stephen, for Jim

From Jim Whitehead I learned a lot about how the great poems of all time ought to be approached: with passion, obsession, and an incredulity that anyone would *not* be stunned. Hearing him read one of those masterpieces, watching him *become* the poem—this was worth the price of admission as a student in the University of Arkansas MFA program in the 1980s.

From Jim, I also learned that writers, even one's teachers, will steal. One day I took a piece of folklore I'd discovered, a formula for curing a fever, into his office and said, "Think that'd make a good poem?" He frowned the famous Whitehead frown and said, "Yeah. And make it more than six lines." He knew, of course, my predilection for writing short poems. He also knew my tendency to procrastinate. As I was leaving, he threw down the gauntlet: "And if you don't write it, I will."

I hied myself that minute to the MFA lounge and began what became, for me, an epic poem—65 lines—titled "For Stephen, Who Owns a Bag of My Cut Fingernails Carried in the Mouth of an Eel Who Swam the Caddo." So, to Jim I say, "Thanks and I'd have sooner come down with chickenpox than let you have that story."

Still, think what Whitehead might have done with those fingernails and eels . . .

For Stephen,
Who Owns a Bag of My Cut Fingernails
Carried in the Mouth of an Eel
Who Swam the Caddo

On out fifteen miles past Wabbaseka,
past Seaton, Gethsemane, and Plain,
he and I grew up neighbors in houses
facing Danner's Bayou. White plantation houses,
splendid except for needing paint.

Except for occasional killings,
times were quiet.
One night the police broke into Mama Laura's place,
the Dew-Drop Inn on 3rd where the black people went.
They found where a fire had been, and bones.
She got the bones, they said, out of graves.
Then my father told me about Vera,
who worked for my mother. He said that's where
they all learned.

We went to her place and hollered till she came out,
scraping the wash-house door.
We begged her to tell us. She told us no.
She said my mama would run her off,
and we were babies.
We were ten and twelve. We loved the way
she smelled.
We wanted to know about the bones.
She said we were evil children.
She said to come back in an hour.

All through high school he and I met at the bayou,
early, before flies.

We tried to do what she'd taught us. We got scared.
One April morning in my senior year,
the moon in its last quarter,
we got it. Except neither of us knew the woman
we made appear.
We scraped the twigs together and watched them burn.

I knew we had the power.
I said we ought to tell Vera,
who'd quit us and gone home.
She died in middle August, during drought.
Neighbors who went in for the body
found in the top of her closet
a little coffin
not much bigger than a shoebox,
with owls' feet and a few thin sticks.

He went to college in Missouri.
I buried Mama and went to work for the bank.
I wrote him drought was ruining Danner's Bayou.
We never got married. It seemed as though we would.
One day I came to be in St. Louis.
Gazing in a storefront, I saw his reflection
in back of mine.
No accident, he said. He caused it.

We often used the power after that.
That time we met in Bonn, that was my doing.
That time in Platte, as the traffic light changed.

It's two years since I saw him last.
Crossing a street in Memphis,
I enter a bar in Portland, Maine.
He is nowhere around.
I freeze to think what's happening in that bayou,

the three sticks crossing,
the owl dropping a stone where the sticks cross.
The awful joy of it. The tooth, the nail, the blazing.
Looking for him, I circle through the bar.
I look in the mirror.
The person I see does not have my face,
and backs away.

MICHAEL HEFFERNAN

Art and Life: To Jim Whitehead

I know you saw that picture of Courbet's
in the Musée d'Orsay, where everyone
is gathering at the grave of some poor fool,
and the grave is at eye-level, in your face.
The coffin's being dragged up with you in it
by an assortment of townspeople in their robes,
sashes, hats, kerchiefs, bonnets, and long looks,
and the day is one great gloom. The coffin's shut
over your face, your secrets, your bare feet.
The hole is open, yawning, freshly dug.
Meanwhile, across the gallery, a mouth
Courbet shaped from a woman's nether parts,
and nothing else, grins at the name he gave them,
L'Origine du Monde. And you laughed out loud.
I never heard you do it, but you did.
A woman with a face no one had seen
and never would again in just that light
had passed along the sidewalk through the rain,
tossing her hair as you stepped out the door
and caught the breeze she shook against your cheek
for the first and last time ever in this life.
I wouldn't try to tell you what you said
under your breath or kept for later on
to tell me, if you had a chance to say it.
There is a sugar maple by your grave,
and a pond across the path that winds around
beside a plot they call *Garden of Love.*
An old man in a black coat has his back turned.

44

Van K. Brock

In Iowa City, Before Arkansas, Jim Once Said

"My writing friends and I, when I lived in Jackson,
would include tidbits that only we would know.
Give readers all they need, then for distraction,
add more for friends, hidden currents, undertow."
A juggler at the Farmer's Market talks about his tricks
casually, while his bowling pins, spheres, knives,
or flaming wands are airborne. It's part of the shtick,
a way to hide those four-hour practices, nightly,
he laughs about while putting his gear in boxes—
all blazes out. The guts of our craft wind through
decades of thickets, in whose twists we find translucent
layers of commonplace or difference to wrap wry secrets.
Whatever Jim was saying, I heard assertions,
in a voice clear and firm—both inquiring and certain.

Jim, the Ozarks are wet and cold. Trees laugh
gold and red in Wilson Park, where Skull Creek
still gurgles toward the Illinois. Above, a sleek
redtail, swooping and soaring, reminds me that
decades ago, I praised you when I heard you'd said,
"we should give our students at least as good as was given
                                                          us,"
when that was not in vogue. And if you dented
heads, I know you helped them discover musics
they might have missed without those elusive nuances,
freeing—from balled-up essences stifling in their marrow—

new clefs. Now, I find you here, where you mined those

                                                       currents

you spoke of long ago—your unfinished furrows
left open on raw hillsides—and in shifting weather
I wish we laughed over these rocky slopes together.

DAVE SMITH

Red Dress

Just to get out of blistering sun, as they do, rummaging,
I walk into the Goodwill Store, and kill some time
on Florida Avenue. Among poor women who waddle
or stand in shade-pools so big a man might roll unseen
like a carp there, I pass under glazed faces blankly
facing west, the sun afternoon's flesh-altering laser.
I see one of them hold it up, calculating, and I laugh

involuntarily, unable to stop my shame rising, caught
as she catches herself in this moment of wanting.
Fire's red, a leaf of gold sequins at each little breast,
fabric a silky, shimmery T-shirt full of wet moves, it
sways in all the ways any slender one might hope.
But I see this too-small cover would howl and scream,
burst and tear in the gripped fingertips of this woman

who grins, now, at me, teeth white as old linoleum.
How it happens I cannot exactly say but Otis Redding
drops to us, humping through pipes, the blue pool
of shade we are in shivers, we are suddenly locked
together, apart, bumping, a mid-aisle twist of hips,
so I remember a man's dancing, his big bear-slide
scarring the floor as he tackled each note and ran off

the night's wiggly minutes. Jim, it is like that today,
shaking this woman in raw pleasure, loving all
Otis gives to the last. Then, in cold sweat, I walk

47

quickly away, pass an aisle of cardboard palm trees,
pass gold fruits by doors to the free sun, but there
I look back, unable to stop myself, and I see how
we grow huge with years of wanting, the blood dress,

tiny as a doll's dream, still hovering before the lips
making it breathe, red as my flushed face, so alive
I gasp as it collapses, crumples, and is disappeared.
Her fat hands wad it down in her bag, restrain it,
tuck it under all she has carried so long. But eyes
flicker as if to sirens where I turn to go, past me,
past hearing what must be only hunger's sucked-in

breath. Or is it the sound, long forgotten, of a tongue's
wet scrape on bare skin, in car-dark, in dim room,
two roped inside music still spinning, of itself only,
inexplicable? Some days all we take is weeping
for what we could not resist, for summer finning
your fingers as you fly in traffic, hot, slick, the way
a dress coils, pushed down, dance done. Some days not.

PHOTOGRAPHS BY BRUCE WEST
Clearings

Clearing for New Houses

The Woods Behind the Houses, #1

The Woods Behind the Houses, #5

The Woods Behind the Houses, #6

From Whitehead

JAMES T. WHITEHEAD

Lecture

If that freshest girl
Comes up to you after class,
Tell her you covered it all in the lecture,
Tell her her teeth are perfect
As are, no doubt, her notes—
Tell her you know she's brushed her hair
A hundred times, like her grandmother did,
And tell the girl she's better than granny.
It's true, for the most part—
Tell her her legs are clean and that
Her feet are chaste—
Tell her to go away . . . .

But if she persists, listen.
She knows the file down at the house
Says Paranoia's box—
The one that says you're hot
For absolutes
And big questions, like *Why*
Did Eliot become a Christian
And leave us in the cold?

JAMES T. WHITEHEAD

For Donald Davidson

The intricate decline of reverence
Is on my mind, old Davidson he knew.
He got the black man wrong, but had good sense
About the wretchedness of what's true.

He heard the century's wind against the gate
As Hardy did. Bird call burned in his mind—
He wrote how unconcerned we build a fate
Absolutely ugly, for being unkind.

He got men wrong from time to time. So do
We all—all races will, if blood is truth.
Watch the most recent fires, call them true.
There is no intricate decline of wrath.

Only kindly reverence for rage
Well turned goes down.
                    Read well before you turn his page.

James T. Whitehead

from Getting To Altamira

At the beginning, having decided to strap on this assignment, I expected to end up writing a violent and cunty article, or at least I wanted to believe it would turn out that way, because somehow I'd been led to believe the Amazon was indeed both violent and cunty, and because I figured most people would enjoy that kind of story.[1] I would enjoy that kind of story.

The original reason for going down there had to do with news reports that described Altamira as a crazy town, crazier even than Texarkana. It had grown, because of Trans-Amazonian adventure, from maybe 2,000 souls to a population of going on 30,000 within a couple of years. Hell raising! Violence and cunt. Super inflation. A hundred taxis would roar up and down the one paved street. An Amazonian Volkswagen demolition derby. The reports described a very large *zona*—fourteen-year-old blonde whores in abundance. And there was one story about the famous Madame Zsi-Zsi who was supposed to operate the largest floating bordello on the Xingu. Soldiers and gun-packing construction workers— hundreds of families of colonists from the Northeastern Bulge passing through Altamira where they're processed and then sent out along the roads into the new communities, into the *agrovillas*—*Agrovilla* John F. Kennedy, *Agrovilla* Abraham Lincoln, to name two we saw.

---

[1] Commissioned by *OUI* magazine in 1973, Whitehead's sixty-page essay was never published. In abridging this piece, we have decided (for readability's sake) to leave cuts unmarked and have added several footnotes using Whitehead's own (excised) words.

When the man from the magazine calls you and asks you to go out on the road from Altamira in the Amazon, you go.

The Amazon is your basic adventure. Piranhas—my imaginations of the Amazon have always included piranhas. I remember movie shots of an oxen in a stream being reduced to bones in a minute—and there was the story that Eric Fleming, the Gil Favor of the old *Rawhide* series, had been eaten by piranhas while on location in the jungle. Plus the savage driver ants that can tear away a jungle almost as fast as a Caterpillar bulldozer.

I'd also read Joseph Conrad's great tropical novels, maybe my favorite books—*Nostromo, The Heart of Darkness, Lord Jim* and *Victory*—and before I left I read *Tristes Tropiques* by Claude Lévi-Strauss, which is a great work of anthropology and literature. I'd published a novel about a South Mississippi boy who was obsessed with pine barrens and swamps, obsessed with how his emotions got confused and embarrassed by his love for both rank nature and pussy.

I had to go.

And I was lucky enough to go with friends, Roy and Dr. Bill, though I didn't know either one of them very well before we went.

Swarmin' in Belém—
Drinkin' rum and tetracycline—
Swimmin' in the Rio Amazon—
When I get home
I'll be a better father, husband, son.

Bill and Roy and I had written the first American-Amazonian country song back at the São Geraldo before we went to see the consul. We'd had us a drink of the finest rum in the world (104 proof Montilla that tastes like the memory of good loving), had written our song and gone off to get our papers in order, which you see we did—but the next plane to Altamira didn't leave until New Year's Eve Day (though maybe we didn't get clear of the consul until the 28th—his letter is dated the 27th).

Onward—we tried to do Belém before we left, and by the day before New Year's Eve Day, Dec. 31, 1973, which was a Sunday, we felt good about the trip so far and our prospects once we got to Altamira—so decided to go out to the Island of Mosqueiro. There were soccer matches in the city but Roy said it might be more interesting on the island. It was about a hundred miles downstream toward the saltwater.

Earlier in the week I'd asked some people whether they'd ever seen the fabled *pororoca*, a tidal bore, an extraordinary wall of water ten or more feet high that rises and pushes up river with the freshwater tides sometimes. Nobody said they'd seen it, but one man said he'd heard its roar one night while he was fishing.

Roy said there would be a three-foot freshwater surf on the far side of Mosqueiro and people in the bars said it was the right place to go before Altamira. The fisherman also believed in the Trans-Am, but said there was too much *bangee bangee* out on the road and then handed me a copy of the Belém paper, *O Liberal*, that carried a story of a shooting outside Altamira. A man walking west on the highway had been shot down from a distance, apparently from the jungle off across the field, and the authorities hadn't found the killer, but they were looking.

Roy thought it was probably a hunting accident. Bill said this was danger, not adventure.

Good, I thought, bring on the *bangee-bangee* from Altamira (a stupid and cruel attitude) and I hope the runway at Altamira is covered with blonde whores, thicker than massed starlings. Because sometimes in Belém those four days I knew already I'd bitten off ten times more than I could chew in nonfiction—what I'd finally do in a couple of years would be a novel that ended up down here. One insane textbook salesman, one country music star, and one crop-duster—all of whom I'd written about before, in a sketch of the book—would come to Amazonia for the same reasons there are thousands of other American men along these rivers, men who have chucked it for a brown mistress or two and a fair-sized launch to live on and fish from. Shit. Half the men in the world are coming down here to make money and the other half are here to forget the life that made them rich and miserable enough to run off.

I'd written about Taggart and Travis Belfontaine and Caldwell Bobo long before I met me or Roy or Bill down there—hell, I didn't even know Roy or Bill when I started *Coldstream.*

Taggart would lead a pair of oxen and a calf down to the river near the mouth, where there were piranhas—he'd drive them into the water to watch their death, and then he'd join them as the *pororoca* swept upstream with the sound of cannons—maybe it was true that a person can be destroyed from the neck down, possibly even for a minute survive a stopped heart and a broken spine, and be awake to study how his flesh is carried off by these natural fish at the moment when his skull is pitched up to the full moon (they say the *pororoca* always comes with a full moon) by a wall of fresh water.

It wouldn't be my skull, not mine.

In *Nostromo* Conrad writes of his character Decoud: *Decoud caught himself entertaining a doubt of his own individuality. It had emerged into the world of cloud and water, of natural forces and the forms of nature. In our activity alone do we find the sustaining illusion of an independent existence as against the whole scheme of things of which we form a helpless part.*

Pretty fucking fancy, but also true enough sometimes. And what has that to do with how *Love without Jealousy is like a Flower without Perfume* is pasted above bus driver seats in Brazil?

The northern Brazilians seem to understand that all the nature around them will eventually smother them like an ignorant father and an ignorant mother. They sense that nature will kill them—and sense that maybe their government in cahoots with the globals means to kill nature—but, still, their lives and their music are about their own intelligent understanding of romantic love, which romantic love is not your bad-assed kill-your-truelove-with-a-shotgun redneck American love—or your savage-your-ex-spouse-in-divorce-court American middleclass love. What I saw of the Brazilian versions seems less hysterical than what we do.

They seem to realize that human beings don't easily come to terms with nature. Either it eats them alive or they kill it. I won't say they're sensitive to ecology, because most aren't.

Brazilian lovers are jealous of each other because they know that nature isn't capable of jealousy because jealousy says you are absolutely individual and I need you in a way that defies the general animal need to merely procreate, though they are great with children. Jealousy is the most essential way to be civilized between the jungle and the sea. It says *I I I* and *you you you*.

So Brazilians don't often kill for love the way we do. There is too much death around already. Nature takes care of that.

On the other side of the island we ate a meal of fried beef, farina, and vegetables on the patio of the Hotel Farol. The wind was up and the freshwater surf was high and the beach stretched out of sight to either side of us. We drank our beers and ate (now and then a gust would shake the bottles on our table and blow farina on our shirts) and watched a middle-aged man with a young woman down on the beach just below us. They were horsing around, touching each other a lot, but we couldn't agree as to whether she was his daughter, his mistress, or his wife. You couldn't tell by the way they kissed. I was thinking mighty fine, mighty fine, and feeling good, less and less concerned about the perfume of jealousy and the strange *pororoca* until I realized the closest continent to us was Africa and that these two continents had once been one mega-continent—how on the map they look like huge pieces of a puzzle. Shit. I was maundering again and suffering an attack of the fall-apart on my central nervous system.[2]

I would come back down here next year and write the novel in a second story room in the Farol, or, better, I wouldn't leave today, because I realized how tired I was and how I never wanted to move again. On a pleasant island of cottages between the jungle and the narrow ocean why would anyone wish to leave? Also, for a couple of minutes while I figured my identity was breaking up in all the most commonplace tropical ways, I was positive I understood why those people were out there building their nine thousand miles of roads. Very very simple. Fortunes would be made for sure and a million farmers would be given two hundred and fifty acres (a hundred hectors) or so of land that leaching rains would often destroy (the children of the farmers probably would grow up to work on the gigantic company farms that would be established behind them on either side of Trans-Am, or in the mines or mills or cane factories) and the roads *would* serve a military purpose — they'd later use them to put down democratic and/or socialistic revolutions in other countries, because, by God, the U.S. and Brazil were the United States of North and South America and all the freaking ships at sea

---

[2]   Elsewhere, Whitehead explains: "Bill said something about the Brazilian *fall-apart*, a disease we had playfully imagined while we were getting every goddamned shot imaginable back in Fayetteville—cholera, typhus, tetanus, yellow fever, malaria, and gamma globulin to ward off hepatitis. To name a few. But Bill imagined, back home, that there was no shot to protect us from the *fall-apart*, a disease that attacked the central nervous system and then caused your extremities to slough off."

and together would rule our hemisphere hey hey hey—BUT that's not why we were in the fucking jungle.

Am I going to agree with noted women's liberationists who say that all agriculture is a form of rape *in the minds of men* and that we must *stop* thinking of the earth as female, which is the cruelest chauvinistic myth? Shall I entirely reject my metaphor of cunt? Call the Green Hell our lungs but lordy not a cunt, and for goodness sake reject the idea that to the minds of troubled explorers the waters of the rivers are a terrible menstrual flow. Something like that. What are the *sapopemba* trees if we think that way, the *jatobas*?

I agree . . . .

We suffer from too many sexist metaphors—although they're not going away any time soon.

The Trans-Am is *not* merely a study in greed, nor is it merely an awful Texas rough-fuck of the basin. Nope. Or at least I was positive out at the Farol on Mosqueiro.

And, dear reader, it isn't a matter of climbing the mountain because it's there. No way.

It's not *macho*, because it's just as much *femmo*. Some of the strongest and most professional new Brazilian women have gone to work for INCRA in the jungle.[3]

Say it, goddamnit, Whitehead.

Friends (*male and female, say the cells*), what they're doing in there is probably the last great exercise in Liberal Optimism the world will see. It's either the last, or the first great success. They believe in Western Civilization, friends—they believe

---

[3] Whitehead explains: "You go to Altamira because of *Trans-Amazonica*—because Altamira is now a *ruropolis* on *Trans-Amazonica*, so defined by the fancy rhetoricians of INCRA, the Brazilian colonization and agrarian reform agency. . . . You go to Altamira because the Brazilian military dictatorship (since 1964) and the multinational global corporations are opening Amazonia to exploration, colonization, and exploitation—they consider *Trans-Amazonica* to be possibly the equal of the American space program in spite of negative criticism that says: *They're building roads to link the poverty of the Northeastern Bulge with the misery of the jungle . . . .* They're in there dynamiting and shoveling their way through the Green Hell."

61

they have learned something from history—they believe that they are semi-rational and that they are *not* controlled by a death wish. And the Brazilians believe they are the most civilized people in the world. Listen—the Brazilians believe they are the *most* civilized people in the world. True, they have an inferiority complex because no Brazilian has won a Nobel Prize and they do tend to worship Pelé like maniacs, but on the balance they think they *are* balanced.

Their architecture *is* brilliant and architecture *is* the test of civilization. They *are* Catholic but not fanatically—they allow for freethinking in religion (though not in politics) and also *macumba* rites. They have the greatest popular music in the world, a music that is to be heard but also to be danced to, which is very civilized (I am not being ironic).

No country in the world is so perfectly balanced between the best optimisms of European Civilization and the slowly disturbed nihilism of gross nature and primitive culture with all its vision.

What we saw down there was a belief in progress and a willingness to create a new mythology. They—who in the hell are *they?*—*they* are the best sentences by the best people we met when they were at their best. They believe they can rationalize the jungle by way of technology and commerce, while providing a style of life that is sensual. They believe they can use the jungle without killing it.

Blank nature is *inhuman and repellent*—I think the poet Elizabeth Bishop said that. *Where man is not, nature is barren*—the poet Blake said that—also, the cold mechanical eye of machinery is repellent.

Brazil is a nation of mixed races, at best.

They are building *Trans-Amazonica* because they (the Brazilians who are *using* the global corporation) mean to show the tight-assed asexual capitalists how to put a skin on a log chain, because they mean to show the Communists

62

an organized civilization that need not deny our dreams of responsible individuality.

They'll also pull out your fingernails and bury you in shit and support the torture of Chilean patriots. Some in power do.

Will it work? I doubt it. Nature is more ignorant and subtle and persistent than they imagine—and civilization with its sweet farts of reason is subject to the short lives of humans and to the confusion and rust of machinery.

On the Island of Mosqueiro I re-affirmed my belief in the essential fuckedupedness of humans and also in a quaint tragic view of life.

I said to Bill, "I'll do this right in fiction."

He said, "This is an article."

Then the German lady from the tour boat showed up. She was glad to see us. She said, "Tomorrow you go to Altamira."

I truly shudder to think how things might have gone in Altamira had we not gone down to the São Lucas about that time—maybe we would have found her later, but maybe not. Whatever, in the hard sunlight of late morning we stepped into the store. Roy negotiated with the good-natured druggist who handed me a big blue and white can of powder. The druggist said he was pleased to see some Americans in town—we'd come at a good time, he said, because of the dances tonight—at which point we heard the loudest sound we'd heard or would hear in Brazil: GRINGOES—GRINGOES. The words were rolled and trilled, were chanted, and the young brown woman had taken over the store and us in about ten seconds from a standing start. She and Roy were talking Portuguese so joyously I was sure she had to be a woman from Cuiabá he'd known before, but she wasn't[4]—she was from Belém, recently come to Altamira, and was the INCRA dentist.

O Lord of Vegetation and Insects—of Piranhas and Tapirs, I thought—O Lord I know whatever positive powers exist down here have sent this woman to us—please don't let her go away.

"She's Teri," said Roy, introducing us. "Jim's writing and Bill's a doctor."

Bill produced a warm handshake while doing a brief, jubilant shuffle with his healthy feet.

I said, "Hey hey hey" to Teri. To Roy I said, "Buddy, this has got to be our good luck. She'll carry us through."

Roy agreed, and Teri, without English, understood how much I appreciated her. She squeezed my hand like a sweet den mother.

Across the street in the café with no name, we were drinking beer and talking about ourselves. What a mouth she had and how she did dance her sentences across her agile tongue—she wanted to know who we were—she wanted to hear about medicine in the States—music and poetry, too—and she asked us if we wanted to go to the big dance at Brazil Nova with her tonight.

Tell her "we do—we do," said Bill to Roy.

We stopped to help a fellow colonist change a tire. I helped lift the Volkswagen out of the ditch and then walked into a field for about fifty yards, toward the trees.

I took deep breaths. I took more deep breaths. I felt like crying. But I didn't. I let out a yell. Noise! Jesus. I wanted to hear my own noise. OOOOM-GAWWA-MATSI-MATSI.

---

[4] Whitehead explains: "Because the word was around that I was going to the Amazon, Roy showed up at my office one day and said he knew Portuguese and was interested in getting back to Brazil. He had learned Portuguese as part of his Peace Corps training, had already lived two years in Mato Grosso, had come back to finish a chemical engineering degree so he could get a good job when he returned to Brazil where life was generally better than here. The music better, and the women more beautiful, especially the women of Cuiabá."

From back on the road some men yelled a response to me. They seemed to believe I had the right attitude.

Glory! I shouted, getting back on the bus—watching our desperate driver begin to aim again.

Bill said he was glad he'd come along, which made me feel better because Betty, his wife, had said in Fayetteville, "He sometimes wanders off . . . please, don't let him."

What could I do if he wandered off right now? Send a wire back home through Belém, a phone call—BILL HAS WANDERED OFF, SORRY?

Once in Brazil Nova we were not disappointed. On the second of January when we came back to do business we saw the new town in hot sunlight—but on New Year's Eve all there was was the big social club building, the country club for administrators, engineers and technocrats—and it looked *great*. We got there about 11:30 p.m. and I could feel the pleasure building.

These were civilized people, citizens of São Paulo, Rio, Porto Alegre, Salvador (where the best Carnivals are held)— these were the best the dictatorship had to offer. They'd left the best beaches in the world to serve time for . . . *for the people?* FOR THE FUTURE OF BRAZIL.

The jungle was a cause—it was a reason to believe they were the only people left in the world capable of balancing sensuality and reason.

Teri had convinced me.

I'll go back.

Everything had convinced me.

Inside the social club building were at least a hundred people and the samba band was wired and good enough—the police whistle was blowing, which sounded like the whistle at roller rinks in America when it's time to change partners. Bill pointed out what the police whistle sounded like.

All three of us agreed that this was worth writing about— the dancing began to ease my mind, or soften it.

Everything was brown and green in the social club and it took Roy half an hour to get up with Teri. I said, "Roy, goddamnit, this is your music—this is the music that freed you from the tight-assed Ozarks."

When he did get up he was comfortable. He moved with Teri like the marriage of northern Europe and Africa. She pulled him to his feet and they moved in front of each other like shy children who want to share a massive secret.

At the Carnival New Year's Eve celebration in Brazil Nova you dance with the entire community. Face to face you dance and then you join a line of dancers that includes everybody from fifteen to sixty.

State the obvious—mix Africa and Europe and we might have something worthy of Asia—let's hear it for the mixed blood of Northern Brazil.

As I stepped from the john I heard yelling, loud but small yelling. There were, say, a half dozen men in loose-flowing tropical shirts lined up along the back wall of the foyer. Each held a beer bottle and each swung the bottle back against the wall to smash it as if he were a member of the chorus in *West Side Story*—the glass broke and they rushed out the front doors chasing somebody.

I followed them into the yard of the social club. In the dim light outside I could see men running across a wide field toward the jungle.

Gunshots—*bangee-bangee*.

Out on the lawn people chattered and wrung their hands—the gunshots were swallowed up by the huge sky and the trees that stood around.

Something had happened.

Those men who ran off into the woods meant to cut someone a new one. *Violence*, I thought. *Cunt*, I thought. The spirit of violence is chasing somebody into the cunt—but it didn't work.

It was probably no more than a fight at a VFW dance in Vicksburg. Not exactly. The defenders had organized themselves swiftly to strike down a threat to INCRA.

Back inside I sat down at our table beside the dance floor where the high strung guitars and police whistles were going on as if nothing had happened. I sat down in a slat chair. It collapsed. I was on the floor with broken sticks around me. Then, quickly, there was a host of Brazilians around me, helping me into another chair.

Had they been watching me?

Was it because I weighed 275 lbs. or because I was an investigative reporter?

Teri and Roy came over to laugh at my embarrassment in a friendly fashion—but I did not feel friendly. I knew better. I was sure of what I'd seen. The man who was dying in a dark slough in the jungle was a revolutionary! Who he was was a man against this profanation of human and natural resources. The man who'd been run off was the last hope of Amazonia, so I had decided. For a moment.

I told Roy to ask Teri what was going on.

Roy looked at me with his hardest Ozark eyes—he said, "What happened wasn't important."

Dance—Teri said for me to dance.

I was drunk and growing pissed. "No, man. I want to know what that was all about."

Roy said we'd never know, exactly. He was not exactly correct but I accepted his opinion for the time being because what I wanted to do was dance more. Sure enough.

Lord did we samba, with the young and the old. I danced with the girl called "the snake," the tallest blackest girl in Altamira—I bopped in a circle with an old couple from Belém who were serving their country, the *world's most successful dictatorship—the world's most sensual dictatorship.*

Again I was homesick for where I was.

Obrigado—Obrigado—Obrigado.

The drummer for our dance was good and the singer wasn't about to wear out. I broke a whiskey sweat and didn't leave the floor until it was grey dawn outside. The party was over at sunrise. I vaguely remember the hammering we took during the ride back to Altamira. I powdered myself again in the hotel and wondered what kind of night the freedom fighter was having in the jungle.

Along the Trans-Am the *agrovillas* had names, such as *Agrovilla* John F. Kennedy, but the place we went to was nameless, a cleared space with thirty small houses, about half of which were in use. No church. No social club—and a Brazilian town without a social club is very primitive indeed.

We stopped at a house where three women stood on the porch—a white woman, a *moreno*, a black.

Their men were in the fields and, yes, it was better here than where they'd been before. One said, "Land is like people—it grows old and dies. This was new land."

I asked if they missed . . . if they missed a larger town. The question didn't register.

I asked if they feared the jungle at night. They said they had fire and light in their houses.

Alfredo was studying me as I questioned them. I'm positive he knew this community wouldn't survive out here, but he never would admit it.[5]

Bill took pictures of those women and when I study them I know I never understood *Trans-Amazonica.*

Our last day in Altamira we walked the town with Teri, took pictures, visited in the cafés and bars—there was all kinds of street work going on in town. The water and sewer system was being expanded. We got drunk that night with a

---

[5] Whitehead explains: "We went back to Brazil Nova to do journalistic business. Once again the consul's letter worked—we were given . . . a driver and a beat-up Volkswagen at INCRA in Altamira. We were off to see the director of everything for miles around—Alfredo—who turned out to be the first person to pick me up when I flattened the chair the other night."

couple of young men and women who were either on the extreme Left or the extreme Right in Brazilian politics. We couldn't tell. They jacked us around and seemed to be frantic to explain something they couldn't. They ended up angry at us because we were getting out the next day.

"You love our music?"

"Right."

"You think we are cruel."

"I haven't seen any . . . ."

"We are a crazy people to be here."

"If you say so."

One fellow who'd lived in Detroit for two years was especially hostile, saying in English—"You can't understand how much we have."

Bill had wandered off—and Roy said he ought to walk Teri home. She was sorry about the arguments but said not to worry; she'd say goodbye in the morning. She said I'd seen enough.

We flew to Manaus because we'd been told it was the place to end our trip—but it didn't amount to much. Or maybe it's another story.

In Manaus we spent our time talking about Belém and Altamira. Bill said he'd had a good time but was ready to go home. Roy said he was sorry to see us go—but he'd be happy to go down to Cuiabá in Mato Grosso where he had other friends and where he'd look for work. I said I was in trouble. I said it would be a long time before I understood this jungle and these rivers.

On the flight from Manaus to Bogotá across the jungle again for hours and hours, I drank and looked down at the trees and the rivers. I drank and drank, but I couldn't get drunk. I tried to remember Teri and Alfredo, the Island of Mosqueiro, everything—but for hours all I saw was the jungle and the jungle didn't know my trouble or my name.

JAMES T. WHITEHEAD

Apology

If only you hadn't had that thirty-eight
Beside you on the seat, we'd have surely made it . . . .

Yes, it had to do with incidents
In town your father feared, but all events

Near violence disturb my equilibrium—
And in your car it squatted there as glum

As your father's leather eye, a cruel of steel.
Woman, soft and soft, it made me feel

I was amuck in every alley. My prey
Was you. And worse—you were just then away

From where we kissed, were in that alley set
To stop me in my tracks. It made me hot.

I was afraid you'd kill the other me
With the other you, your father's dear, his lady.

JAMES T. WHITEHEAD

from Coldstream

1.

Today is the day I decided that soon I must marry and breed, do right and get down to where the human race is, because the beautiful widow Chalet Bobo has called and got through to me here at the Bigger Bee Motel in Putman, Mississippi. It is Sunday morning, heirs, and I am about where the coastal meadows and the piney woods come together on Highway 49—and the Necases who run this awkward, troubled court have been told they ought not put anybody through to my cabin unless it is my father or my mother, both of whom are old and depend on their wayward son for entertainment— but Dutch Necase probably broke his promise because Chalet's voice is sweet and low—"is this the motel where Coldstream Taggart is hiding from his friends?" "Why, yes ma'am it is. Would you like for me to rouse him up?" "I most surely would, thank you."—her voice is sweet and low, is skillfully modulated Delta speech with the least salt of hysteria in it. Chalet calls to report that she and her son Roger and her daughter Laura for the first time got drunk together night before last in the kitchen of their comfortable home that is out from Pernicious, Mississippi, and that in the midst of their ongoing grief—better than three weeks of it by now—she broke down completely and told those marvelous young people that their daddy did not exactly drown in the waters of the mighty Amazon. Sweet Bobo was not exactly swept slowly away into the estuary of The River Sea. I have tried to imagine how his body might have looked

71

as it turned and rolled along the bottom of the river if he had actually drowned—but he didn't—and she told Laura and Roger what really happened *so far as she knows*.

Belfontaine, Royal and I had wanted to protect Bobo's family from the full catastrophe, had managed to keep the truth from Chalet and all the others for better than twenty-four hours after we got back home with no Bobo, with no promise that the body would follow shortly after us by air freight, and with no bones. We'd told them he drowned while fishing alone in the morning, and we'd meant to keep the rest of it among ourselves forever. Obviously we didn't.

Therein lies the tale, I'm sure, and what has recently motivated me to breed.

Laura and Roger seem to have enjoyed the excitement of getting drunk with their mother, no matter how terrible her story was, but the fact that their father's friends did not stay around to dive for his bones has made them furious. "Hurt and furious," Chalet said.

"No dead body at the funeral is serious business, and no bones when there might have been bones is worse, I suppose," I answered. "There's no doubt about it."

Roger has gone off to Memphis to talk about death and rituals with the famous anthropologist Valparaiso Gomez who has recently converted himself into a broker for the time being and has moved into an office tower until he makes the million dollars necessary to finance the outdoor research he wants to do for the rest of his life. Laura, equally serious, has decided to move in with her father's protégé spraypilot, Bertram, that bronze boy, for the time being. Chalet is naturally upset by these events but she is not about to harm herself on account of them. She only wanted to tell me.

We told Chalet about how he drowned, and then how we dove and dragged for him—then how, when all else failed, we waited for his body to surface, putting around the Amazon for a day and a night and a day in our Brazilian johnboat.

"He loved the Amazon and it will do just as well to leave him there, toucans and curassows lamenting. Almost a pastoral elegy," I told her. Then later on we told her a version that is much closer to the truth, is absolutely accurate about the cause of death, if not the fully orchestrated performance of it, or the reason. Heirs, I honestly don't know the reason he did it, or it happened.

We had this conversation with her at dawn out on the runway that lies between the house and the hangar— BOBO'S FLYING SERVICE SPECIALIZING IN AERIAL APPLICATION. His three friends lost control and told his wife that he was eaten by piranhas.

It was quite a scene out there on the runway with the full moon still brightly visible and the sun about to take the horizon. The four of us took an oath to keep the manner of Bobo's death a secret—this after Chalet had gone somewhat to pieces thanking us for telling her the truth. We all cried together and then embraced one another because of what we'd sworn, but of course her telling her children about the fish was inevitable and changes everything, making your lives possible. The truth will out and now that Roger and Laura are possessed of their terrible vision, many stories about how Bobo bought it will get around to everybody from here to kingdom come. It is a destiny by now and so it has come to pass that I must marry and breed. Strap it on. Strap it on.

It was Judge Royal Carle Boykin, Travis Belfontaine (the country music star), and I who saw it happen. Seeing it was awful but hearing it was essential—elemental—almost beyond my powers of description. Bobo's cry was torn from so deep in his brain it seemed that we were present at the creation of the world, or the end of it. I have practiced trying to make that sound many times since then but I'm sure I've never got it right. His scream caused me to go deaf for awhile directly after I heard it, and, for hours at a time, since. *AIIIII—YEEEE—HA—AHA*, cried Bobo from the water after he grimaced—or grinned—God knows—when he was first aware the fish had struck him.

Children! Get down! Caldwell "Lurch" Bobo was eaten by piranhas just off the *Ila Dos Cavallos* not far from the mouth of the Amazon and his widow Chalet had no trouble finding me here at the Bigger Bee Motel, even though I'd told my parents to keep my whereabouts a secret for awhile. She managed to get through my parents—my mother to be exact—in order to reach the Necases who control the switchboard in the office, which is astonishing. *Almost no one in the world to keep a secret.* Not even my reverent and complicated Momma—and I had done my best to make it clear to her that I had been astonished far too often lately.

Heirs, it is true enough that the capacity to be astonished is a great gift and a great blessing, and true enough that astonishment, along with a sense of humor, is what keeps most people from slowly and intentionally wasting themselves or blowing themselves away with a quick explosion—but I had had your God's plenty of astonishment, I thought—and even if humor is the new religion, I was fresh out of smiles, I told my parents.

Heirs, I was *down.* I'd seen my dear friend slaughtered in the water while on what was meant to be a *lark* along the Amazon, and since I'd returned, I'd had little opportunity to recover. When Bobo went under I thought to myself, "Well, this may be the day of the Lord." Then I thought again: "But not likely. *Perhaps today.* But not likely—for the day of the Lord is a darkness, not this strange brightness and flashing water of an equatorial morning."

And I have never desired the day of the Lord. I have taken the prophet Amos seriously, who said—*Woe unto you that desire the day of the Lord! To what end is it for you? The day of the Lord is darkness and not light.*

As if a man did flee from a lion, and a bear met him; or went into his house, and leaned his hand on the wall, and a serpent bit him.

74

Shall not the day of the Lord be darkness, and not light? Even very dark, and no brightness in it?

2.

I didn't know what to make of Bobo's terrible cry or that ecstasy of fins fluttering on the surface of the bright water. Didn't and don't yet, in any fashion that is comprehensive. *I resisted the zebu idea from the outset.* He'd meant to knock the zebu in the head or shoot it dead before he threw it—pushed it—down the knoll into the creek where the piranhas were. He and Francisco, our guide, had been tossing bits of non-fatty beef to the fish for at least two days—he meant to sacrifice the cow but he never got her in. The rest is history. I resisted the plan but I did far too little to stop it.

To put it very weakly, my circuits were blown out and a fair part of my mind was shut down immediately—even though I was in fact made to understand that this was *not* the day of the Lord, no matter how extraordinary it was. If there is anything my father has tried to teach me it is that every death is one at a time for the most part. There is no doubt that megadeath, when it comes of earthquake or tidal wave, plague or war or drought or whatever, is monstrous and impressive, and the willful killing of a planet is most monstrous of all—but my father, who is a retired Methodist minister, is a Personalist and wants to keep each individual's mortality in focus. He is especially fond of a line from a poem by Baby Leroy, the Basking Poet of North Texas— "Mortality, who would have thought it!"

The point being that people who look forward to The day of the Lord or any other species of apocalypse are, deep down, both murderous and suicidal, which, as I've suggested, is not the worst of it. Oh they may talk about their raptures and about how they won't be possible until the whole gospel is preached throughout the whole world, and so make a great to do about satellite communications and the

Jews' return to the Holy Land, the fig tree in bloom again, but deep down in every apocalyptic heart is rancor and envy, you better believe it, fucking *Ressentiment*, to use Nietzsche's great word. "Spiteful, vicious, sons of bitches," says my father who has seen, but cannot accept the reality of, female apocalyptic. "*Rapture* indeed," he says—"straight to heaven like a rocket or an evaporated mist indeed," he goes on. He has never gone quite that far while in the pulpit, but he has said that people who have an itch for The Second Coming are not likely to learn much from the deaths that are near at hand: say a common highway accident where an entire family is spilled out on the cement or asphalt in a slow rain, their bodies torn and bleeding worse than might happen at the hands of a semi-professional torturer, the mother crying and dying among the fragments of her children. From his pulpit I've heard him cry, "And what about that family, these deaths—we all know it happened not five miles from here. Will you multiply that darkness, that sadness, that pain?" The sort of sermon that will put my troubled mother back on the sauce for months on end.

Apocalyptics are world haters and this is agreed upon by all my friends who grew up in my father's church in Bryan, Mississippi. Your born again people, no matter what desert religion they come from, are very dangerous to life on earth. They hate their present lives and so on down the line . . . .

You finally get down to it and all of it is ego, egos like those actual little fish, and speaking of deep water, and the sound of deep water, I am now in it. For how can I claim that an unconscious fish shall represent a hopeless but conscious ego? Well, of course it is merest analogy, because among humans you can't, so far as I know, have persons without egos. Anyway not very often around here. They face the bear and suddenly realize that they are bit by the serpent, and so conclude that the only way out is to *become* a bear, a serpent, an eagle, a piranhas, slurring all the while the beasts they imitate. How about *that* old saw?

Surely one reason I have feared marriage and the family, along with almost every other responsible human activity, is because I'd absolutely have to come to terms with weighty issues. A scattering of advice hither and thither is one thing, but raising children is quite another.

If someone had come up to me on a street in Belém, or in the café of the São Geraldo Hotel, or the patio of the Hotel Farol on the Island of Mosqueiro, asking me to describe my experience in Amazonia in terms of the senses, I probably would have emphasized the visual, tactile, and the olfactory—green, to be sure, because Christ God, that's what you see and what it is, to say nothing of how it has been called the Green Hell forever, green and all the vivid, most vivid, other colors, especially the unnaturally gaudy mechanical ones flung across fields of green, the high jungle wall of green (it is as if the green of the Southeastern United States were raised by a power of ten)—a regular sensation of being touched by the atmosphere, touched all over by way of something generally sensuous rather than explicitly sexual, I think; although a first boyhood experience of slipping into a lubricated condom does come to mind—and the smell of it all is also tactile, like avocado spread, which appeals more directly to the sense of touch than to the sense of smell. Someone who strolled up to a café table and asked of the senses might have got that sort of answer. Bobo was our interpreter, he was the one who had learned the language well enough to use it before we went down there—*I would have had to think twice before I mentioned sounds*—the patter of Volkswagen motors and the equatorial Portuguese, lilting, fantastically pitched, a beautiful language I'm working on; and I have wondered whether the strain of learning a new language in less than a year might have damaged Bobo, no matter how gifted he was. Because we know now that he was hearing voices long before our trip, the result, Chalet believes, of Dioxin poisoning—Agent Orange.

He'd sprayed in Vietnam and had come home to make his living doing much the same thing. I came into his sunken study and office there at his house a couple of times when he had the earphones on and was studying his language tapes, following along in his text, *Modern Portuguese*; he'd be reciting with great effort—*sei, sabe, sabemos, sabem*—that sort of thing—and the time I best remember, looking down into the dim light of the study and office (Bobo always kept the blinds pulled and rarely turned on more than one of those insect-like reading lamps that sat on the wide arm of his recliner), he was saying his Portuguese out loud while also shaking himself from time to time, violently riffling the pages of his book, and once or twice he said quite audibly, "WHOAH, GET DOWN, HOSS, NO, SHIT NO, YOU . . . HAVE . . . GOT . . . IT . . . WRONG—AAAA—"

Little did I know about what was going on inside of his head, that's for sure. Chalet, because she is beautiful, intelligent, and wise, will be the only person who will ever get close to why he died and *she* won't ever be able to do it until one of us lets out in more detail the fact that it well might have been a suicide. *Did he slip from the knoll or did he dive backwards from it?* Belfontaine, who presently hates Bobo because he's convinced he *used* us, believes it was a carefully prepared and brilliantly brought off suicide—*deeply cynical*—"Why else would he study so hard to learn Portuguese?" Travis argues. And I say, "What the hell has learning Portuguese got to do with it?"

"Hal," he says, "you dumb son of a bitch. You poor observer."

Well of course that sort of reasoning is not fair at all and shouldn't be given the least attention, but for the life of me I can't deny that Belfontaine is Belfontaine—*God, we die and are reborn each day*—Royal Carle believes it was an accident because Bobo was so vain—"Bobo never would have meant to destroy that body he'd worked on for such a long time, unless, Bubba, right up on front street, he *was* out of his mind, and I don't believe he was."

The music? The samba? That, heirs, is a good question. How in the name of goodness could a person be asked about his Brazilian experience and not say that the samba is a great part of it? He could if the samba was a great problem for him. Maybe the greatest. And if the person in question is lazy then he will turn *away* from the question of the seminal samba, as I wish I could. I have not done the most obvious homework. I have not checked out or ordered through the mails the definitive book on the samba, which surely exists. I have listened to it—Lord, have I ever—I have danced to it, for many hours strung together by those profoundly tacky rhythms no pre-Socratic Greek philosopher could ever have imagined—but then again, who knows? Funky Greek music is as disturbing as any samba. Makes me want to get the hell away from the Bigger Bee Motel and head on over to New Orleans for some shuck and jive. I'm coming around at last. But is popular Greek music as tacky as the samba? Does it also extract from the DNA molecules the same *rich truths* as does the samba? I must pause for Inglenook.

Let me try to explain, by way of a rather simple analogy, why I might have left out *hearing* if I had been asked about my senses in Belém.

One time years ago, say, about while I was a senior in college, I sat down with my Momma in Tupelo, Mississippi, one of those conversations we would sometimes have when Daddy was away at a district meeting of the Methodist Church, or some such thing. Often we would talk about people long dead from one side of the family or the other, or talk about my brother Julian who ran away from home in 1950, about the time of the Korean War, and never returned, after the morning he left the house, having blown a chicken from off a pine tree limb above me with a shotgun. No news at all since he roared away on his motorcycle. No record he ever joined the army. Mother drank a little before Julian's departure, a wild excess for a Methodist preacher's wife, but after it became clear that he was *gone*, she got very serious about your gin. An irrevocable loss, Julian.

Whatever. I was drinking with her in the dead of winter. The weather fit around the little house like an icy mitten, rain turning to sleet, sleet turning to rain, outside, and the Bombay martinis she had fixed were working in my mind like higher trigonometry, causing me to come forward with what I imagined would be a heavy if not intolerable question. I asked her how she'd score her sex life with my father. "How's it been?"

You talk about rancor, you talk about what will give you a foot fetish while also leaving you a chirrupy heterosexual for the rest of your days and nights, well, I asked her and she answered my evil question.

She told me she couldn't remember.

I said, "What?" I was afraid she meant they'd quit.

She's sitting there in her austere, grey little knitting and reading chair, with both hands wrapped around a jelly glass full of chilled Bombay gin (the finest, so don't believe those lies about the stuff in the green bottle), vermouth, and olives. She pours in a half dozen olives with each glassful. My question didn't bother her at all; in fact, it seemed to come as a sort of reprieve from whatever her previous thoughts had been while she was sipping and listening to the *tick tick* of the weather against the window. She says she is aware that she and Daddy have been fairly regular about their intercourse over all these years, as I must have heard often enough— "You never did believe it was bad dreams when your daddy told you that was why I yelled. When you was little."

"Oh yes I did," I said, trying to be jocular and familiar in the midst of an interlude I already realized I wanted out of.

"Well, I *don't* remember any outstanding particulars about the times. I'm pleased most of the time and sometimes I'm not, and maybe being a drunkard helps my attitude"—an observation that drove me down deep into my father's chair, because never before had I heard her come out and name her affliction. And *drunkard* was an especially coarse way to put it because it called to my mind ragged old men in doorways, skid rows, old men fallen into winter ditches where they would shortly freeze to death.

I said to her, "It seems to score out pretty much O.K. Right?"

"Oh yes," she said. "Oh yes—if rolling around with your old daddy was the only problem, well, I'd be in the pink—it's dying that scares the shit out of me," she said.

Again I was surprised at her speech. Shaken and troubled by it. How little we know about our parents is a trite comment but the truth. I pressed on—"Momma, the fact that you can't goddamnit remember surely means that you have very dark inhibitions . . . ."

"Honey," she says, "if you don't have some dark inhibitions about what it is that makes babies then you ought to have your head examined." I remember her taking a tremendous swallow from her extraordinary martini before she went on—"Streamer, the God bidness can sometimes be a pain in the bottom and you yourself think too much about it so you just concentrate on making your grades—remember what you want and forget the rest. Hey." She didn't articulate it quite that well, but that's close to the words. She'd lost Julian and the monster baby, Herschel.

What I've meant to say is that I recollect the samba similar to how Momma does sex, a troubled memory and pleasant, but not very sharp.

WHOAH! GET DOWN!

The redundant samba is profoundly trivial, both trivial and profound—*beep beep beep . . . hump hump hump*—the mad police whistle and deep croaks—frog sounds—and line after line about how excellent it is to be in Bahia during Carnival—and the giddy ululations of Latin hyenas, the hyena being a favorite animal of mine—Belfontaine went down there to study the music, looking to incorporate the insight of it into his country songs, and believe me none of the music was wasted on the old man, Belfontaine, nor was it wasted—ratchet ratcheting—on Bobo who for years had been a samba addict, throwing regular samba parties in the Delta long before he went down there to die. He'd have himself decked out in his frilly white shirt with the full sleeves and his coal black dancing trousers—Chalet herself in a long split dress that shows off her marvelous legs, *slick*, flashing while she's turning in the moonlight—those partners—the piney woods redneck who is the hero of five counties in the Delta —his wife the reigning Queen. Late, late, late, out on Bobo's patio, three, four black couples would show up to revel into the dawn. What fanatics we all were those nights, crazy white people and those expensive Africans, all of us wild to be alive in Pernicious, Mississippi.

But it should be computed that Golden Dorgan, Chalet's father, made it all possible—a miscegenated gathering dancing to the world's most miscegenated music beneath the poisoned Delta stars—that old cynic, Golden Dorgan, who *owns* Pernicious, actually took a negress, Black June Overton, deep into the pecan grove one night to have his way with her. Golden is a widower and June is one of my inconstant lovers—Hamitic in origin, Negro, Arab and other ancestry, straight from a dictionary—a dignified people. Bobo was far removed into his pleasure, his joy, that night of one of his Carnival parties and I don't believe it was delight in my jealousy that made him laugh when Golden took June by the hand and walked into the dark.

Heirs, think of protein. Samba is no more trivial or frivolous than how it was at the moment in the history of the earth when protein was formed for the first time.

The redneck who had arrived, spray pilot extraordinary, and the most beautiful woman the Delta ever produced. Bobo and Chalet. Lord. Lord. Summertime. Bobo's dancing parties are always in the summertime, heirs.

James T. Whitehead

For Jean

The next time I visit I'll take your picture.
I know this verse will never work.
I'll catch you walking with your head turned—
You will be talking easily
With Brian, saying

Jim reminds me of my brother.
Ah, what a pix, and what a phrase!
Now, at last I'm free to claim
My sister got the gracefulness—
I am rough bacchii, which she

Scans perfectly—
Her going is the coral stride and turn
Through loveliness. Observe
Precisely how she speaks from her fine wide mouth—
Watch her large eyes passing carefully

Beyond the foolishness of every line.

James T. Whitehead

For Miller Williams

Your clear mind bends a curious line around
A life as strange as Job's—that scientist
At work in Bedlam's cells—and I've been bound,
A friend with you, for years. You read a fist

I wrote in Nashville once. You said a fist
Might make a poem carefully, and smiled—
Then read your frogs and human Jesus Christ
And the furious anatomy a child

Will learn when decency is shot to hell.
Your sorrow of Enlightenment is brave,
Is often beautiful and darkly cool,
The brilliance of intelligence as slave.

Slave to what? I hear your good mind cry,
Cutting to the bone, where all things lie.

PHOTOGRAPHS BY BRUCE WEST
Gardens

Vegetable Garden

Strawberry Net

Goodman's Garden

Sunflowers

For Whitehead

MILLER WILLIAMS

The Alphabet as Part of What We Are

Some of whom we came from came for a chance.
Others came indentured, others in chains,
to these potential, then united, states,
except for those who crossed the Bering Straits,
but they were immigrants, too, although they came
before there was a colony to name.
We're still astounded to find ourselves here,
children of brave and slave and musketeer,
coolie and buccaneer and wetback,
what we call white and yellow, red and black,
believing in living together and learning to.

Knowing how flesh can fail, minds misconstrue,
we have to wonder how we have come this far
toward what we want to be, being what we are.

Part of what keeps us restless and dreaming ahead
is paper printed with ink, words to be read,
thoughts to be spread about, newspapers and books,
journals and magazines—for lingering looks,
on slow strolls in the garden called the brain,
at long impressions where a truth has lain.

MILLER WILLIAMS

An Unrhymed Sonnet

What is existence? What does it mean to be?
How did existence come to be from nothing?
Is nothing lying still at the core of being?
Why is there life? If life began with God,
did God have a beginning? If God was always,
how did God and always come to be?
If neither began, if they run all the way back,
they run back all the way to what, to when?

If time is a long illusion, what is always?
What bangs itself around the universe?
If this one universe is all there is,
all the more the question wants an answer.

Excuse me. I shouldn't ask these questions here.
Please. Just go ahead and cut my hair.

C. D. WRIGHT

4 *from* 40 Watts

Country Station Poem

It goes something like this: when the dog
lunged she froze he fired at the head

They drove around they came back he wore black
they line-danced they drank they fell down

They swore allegiance to the women who bore them
they cursed the women who bore them

The chambers of the heart opened and shut
they made plans they made plans

Poem With Evening Coming On

a dog has appeared at the gate
for the second day in a row
against a dirty peach sky
a single car wobbles into the sun

Poem In Which Blood Flows

They are like brothers but
they know no filial feeling
and keep things in culverts.
As the tires on their trucks sink
into the heavy loam they spill
out of the pool hall's green light
into a plashing crescendo of blades.

Poem With A Cloudburst

the breath of the father
rises and falls

laundry blowing out of a basket
a gar is wrapped up

in some line the mind of the mother
snags on a compound word

such as horsehair
or cottonwood

on the meaning of the color yellow
it must be Sunday

R. S. Gwynn

These Are the Words

These are the words that you must finally say
When those whose words meant most at last are gone,
Whose own tongues taught your own to turn one way,
Whose own lips spoke the speech you call your own.

The angry words that kept you up till dawn,
That sent you out or called you back from play,
That counted blessings that have mostly flown.
These are the words that you must learn to say:

The cruel words, the truths, the lies that weigh
Upon the facts found and the truths unknown,
Tremors and calms from every holiday.
When those who meant the most at last are gone,

Whose voice reveals the visions you've been shown,
Describes the sky's precise degree of gray,
Hurts harder than the angry stick and stone
Your own tongue taught to twist or turn away?

Their faces fade, but now you know that they
Wore the same face into which you have grown,
The chin, the nose, the brow, the mouth that may
Be moved to speak the words which are your own.

Be gentle with them. Or, at least, betray
Them gently. Let the light you've shone
Upon them cast the clear yet kindly ray.
Let the dead lie and let the dead alone.
These are the words.

JOHN DUVAL

Dover
A translation of *Ballade,* by Charles d'Orléans

Charles the Duke of Orléans (1391-1465) wrote this plea for peace during his
twenty-five years held hostage to the English after the battle of Agincourt. It
was Jim Whitehead who reminded me of the scene in Shakespeare's *Henry V,*
on the eve of that battle so disastrous to Charles and all the French, where
Charles says of the English, "Foolish curs, that run winking into the mouth
of a Russian bear and have their heads crush'd like rotten apples!"

One day as I was looking out toward France
From where I stood at Dover-by-the-Sea
I thought about the pleasure that that land
Beyond the Channel used to give to me.
As I kept looking, sighs started to pour
Out of my heart, although it did me good
To see France, which my heart longs for.

I told myself it certainly made no sense
To sigh at a time like this, when I could see
The road was being readied in advance
For good peace, which can bring good things to be.
Then I felt better than I had before
Although I didn't cease to sigh and look
Toward France, which my heart longs for.

I loaded all my wishes, all my wants
Into the Ship of Hope. Across the sea
I sent them on in haste. "Remember me,"
I begged of them, "remember me to France."
Now God grant us good peace, and quickly, Lord,

So I may have the opportunity
To see France, which my heart longs for.

Peace is a treasure. You can't praise peace enough.
War isn't worth the honor. I hate war!
War has kept me twenty years and more
From seeing France, which my heart longs for.

Ballade

En regardant vers le païs de France,
Un jour m'avint, a Dovre sur la mer,
Qu'il me souvint de la doulce plaisance
Que souloye oudit pays trouver;

Si commençai de cueur a souspirer,
Combien certes que grant bien me faisoit

De voir France, que mon cueur amer doit.

   Je m'avisay que c'estoit non savance
De tels souspirs dedens mon cueur garder,
Veu que je voy que la voie commence

De bonne paix, qui tous biens peut donner;
Pour ce, tournay en confort mon penser.

Mais non pourtant mon cueur ne se lassoit
De voir France, que mon cueur amer doit.
   Alors chargai en la nef d'Esperance

Tous mes souhaits, en leur priant d'aler
Outre la mer, sans faire demourance,

Et a France de me recommander.
Or nous doint Dieu bonne paix sans tarder!
Adonce aurai loisir, mais qu'ainsi soit,
De voir France, que mon cueur amer doit.
   Paix est tresor qu'on ne peut trop louer;
Je hé guerre, point ne la doy prisier;

Destourbé m'a longtemps, soit tort ou droit,
De voir France, que mon cueur amer doit.

Leon Stokesbury

The Lover Remembereth Such as He Sometime Enjoyed and Showeth How He Would Like to Enjoy Her Again

Luck is something I do not understand:
There were a lot of things I almost did
Last night. I almost went to hear a band
Down at The Swinging Door. I, almost, hid
Out in my room all night and read a book,
The Sot-Weed Factor, that I'd read before;
Almost I drank a pint of Sunny Brook
I'd bought at the Dickson Street Liquor Store.

Instead I went to the Restaurant-On-The-Corner,
And tried to write, and did drink a beer or two.
Then coming back from getting rid of the beer,
I suddenly found I was looking straight at you.
Five months, my love, since I last touched your hand.
Luck is something I do not understand.

Leon Stokesbury

To All Those Considering Coming to Fayetteville

Often these days, when my mind holds splinters
like the pieces of the Old Spice bottle
I dropped and shattered yesterday, I think
of other places. It is wintertime now,
and the Ozarks are hushed up with snow
everywhere. They are small mountains, almost
not mountains at all, but rather, with trees
sticking up, they seem more like
the white hairy bellies of fat old men
who have lain down here. What has this to do
with anything? I don't know. Except
it makes me think of snow elsewhere, and what
it would be like to be there. I might drive
across Oklahoma, then on into
New Mexico. I could be there tonight.
The land would be flat, the snow over
everything. The highway straight, and forever
the snow like blue cheese in the moonlight,
for as far as there is, and air, cold air
crisp as lettuce, wet lettuce in the store,
and I would keep driving, on and on.

Michael Heffernan

Speak the Speech, I Pray You

The last of sleep was stolen by the sun.
I got up after saying to hell with it.
I hadn't even put my glasses on,
to see what morning's light had in it yet,
when there I was gawking around the play
about the Danish prince, then poring deep
into the teeming midst of all his whirl
of words that pulled me down to the depths to twirl
round and about the least weed like a rope
tossed from the liner while the Captain turned
to puff his pipe alone with his own face
watching him from the pane beyond the wheel.
This had to do with dreams and how they feel
inside our freed souls in the other place,
whither they have gone to be blessed or burned
in everlasting joy or loss of hope,
though nonetheless wakened from troubled sleep,
exactly how or why the man won't say.
Blinded already by my lack of sight,
I rose in search of ordinary light
the day might lend such of the things I found
along with what the cat shook on the ground.

BETH ANN FENNELLY

The Welcoming: An *Ars Poetica*

Distance was the house from which I welcomed you.

Time, time was the house, and to welcome you
I strung garlands of eggshells and rubies.

Thirsty, I welcomed you, you the salt
sucked from the tips of braids
after running from the ocean of someone else's childhood.

I turned the skeleton key. I welcomed you from the narthex
of invisible churches.

There at the marble bar at the *Folies-Bergère*
I welcomed you in the mirror,
waving my chartreuse tumbler,
wearing my velvet choker, wafting my nocturnal perfume.

On the subway of *extranjeros*
I patted the empty seat beside me.

I foraged for you in welcome. Like a bottlenose dolphin,
I tore sponge from the sea floor
covered my beautiful nose with it and dug between
                                    barnacled rocks.
Yes I welcomed you with my efficient body.

102

I welcomed you from the house of memory,
where I am lonely.

Again I vow not to think about whether you arrived,
or in what state.

Just that I was there, welcoming

with a singed collar, with a bee balmed in amber,
with an oyster cracker, a seashell full of champagne.

I welcomed you from a house of needles.
I welcomed you from the fists of babies.

Standing on the doormat
of my black shadow,
with a beginner's brow, with a hoop of angels,
with the ache of unlit candles,
I welcomed you.

BETH ANN FENNELLY

from Telling the Gospel Truth

The next time a student asks
            how to become a writer, I will say,
Sit in a white room
            without paper
                        and think of the poacher
who shot the wing off the bald eagle.
                        Who must have seen
                        he wrecked his trophy
            and, disgusted,
            did not even offer it
                        a second bullet
                but thrashed off deeper into the forest
wearing his expensive
                forest-colored clothes.

Then
            think of the man from the wild bird sanctuary
                        who found the eagle,
                        sutured its ragged wingstub,
                fed the awkward hopping thing
                        for years.
            And, before it died, harnessed it
                in a hang glider and took it to the mountain
so one last time
            its hollow bones could float
so one last time
      its eyes could scour the forest floor from hunter's height,

so one last time

        its talons could tear the gauzy cloak of sky,

                flying in the face

                    of God,

that one last time.

        Think of the poacher, think of the birder.

    Alternate,

shortening the intervals,

Don't forget to breathe.

When you can hold both of these men

             in the palm of your mind

      at the same time,

             Love,

             come find me,

and teach me.

Snapshots

I was going through some boxes in the garage and found a diary from twenty-five years ago, an artifact of a former existence, almost. It was typed on paper that had started to yellow. I remembered fondly the little Smith-Corona portable electric that I was still using back then, when I first moved to Pittsburgh, before I meet Annie. I was what you might call a struggling artist—actually more of a ne'er-do-well calling himself a writer.

I gathered up the box and the diary and came back into the house through the kitchen and sat in a room we called the library.

Annie is my second wife. She's my age, in her sixties, but with her naturally dark hair and flawless skin she could pass for much younger. I associate all the stability in my life with her. We had been going through the last of her mother's things when I came across this box.

She called, "Are you still in the garage?"

If I should ever need a measure of how my life has changed in twenty-five years, I could take a look at these floor-to-ceiling bookshelves and framed Dufys on the wine-colored walls and cobblestone walkways to the fish pool and then remember the other damp corners I called home after my divorce.

I said, "Do you need help?"

In that other life, I was sleeping beneath an overcoat on a pallet of Wal-Mart quilts on the bare floor of a bare room. Before that, I had lived at the YMCA on a cot with clean sheets, among world-class snorers, and in the roar of a window fan as big as a B-25 propeller. It's no exaggeration to say I had been down and out in those lonely days.

"Oh, you're inside," she said. "No, you were just so quiet."

I said, "Okay. Let me know if you need anything."

I sat on the floor and crossed my legs and took a breath and shuffled the diary's pages until they were in order.

Most of the junk in the garage, where I'd found the diary, had belonged to Annie's mother. Boxes of financial papers and books and old photographs, you know, plus a few rag-tag pieces of furniture. Annie was in another room sorting through some other things we had salvaged after the funeral. Annie's mom died back in September, God bless her. She was ninety-three, bent and crippled-up, but bright as a dollar to the end. From the sepia-tinted photographs I knew Annie's mother had been a beautiful young woman, willowy and stylish, so unlike the dear frail ghost whose hands we held as she died.

I read the first line of the diary: "Here's what happened at the end of the affair with Traci."

These pages chronicled a time before I knew Annie. In twenty years of marriage I had gotten used to thinking of my life as a shared entity with her. Now, suddenly, in my hands, lay a scrap of a world that was not shared, all but forgotten, yes, but mine alone, not blended into any part of my life with my wife. It was a little dizzying to hold. I was reading about myself but it was a self I scarcely recognized.

Traci was a twenty-year-old girl I had dated for a while after my divorce. Well, "dated" may not be just the right word. To be more honest, she was a kid in one of my creative writing classes when I had a one-year appointment at a university in the South. I was forty-three at the time. Let's just admit that those days, newly single and a little desperate, were not my finest, and leave it at that.

It was nice to think of Traci. She was pretty, I remembered—her dark eyes and nut-brown hair, her tiny hands and feet. And of course wise for her age, as all cradle-robberies tend to be.

Traci's last boyfriend before me had been a kid in his twenties who died in a swimming accident. This may account for her vulnerability to being seduced by me, anyhow. (I have at least a thousand things to regret from those days.) The boy's name was Jerry, and he broke his neck diving off a bridge. She had had a photo of him on her dresser, and she talked about him a good deal. Good Lord.

The next lines of the diary reminded me that I had invited Traci to come to Pittsburgh to live with me. Double good Lord. It was one of those details I had pushed to the back of my mind. I had invited a twenty-year-old whom I scarcely knew to move with me to a city I had never been in. Doesn't that say it all? I had been grasping at straws in a whirlwind.

Anyway, that was my plan. She would follow me, newly divorced, to a dying steel town fifteen hundred miles away— her parents lived in Shreveport, Louisiana—and leave behind everything important to her. Even at the time, I must have suspected this plan contained flaws. But there it was. She would finish college while I found us an apartment and started my new teaching job, and then she would join me.

The idea had seemed romantic at the time, like being a struggling writer. I pictured her arriving on a great hissing jingling passenger train, the first cars skimmed with ice, a flash of lighted windows in a Pullman car revealing a gleaming porter carrying a bundle of soiled sheets. Then, Traci, a girl in love standing on a foggy platform in a drizzling rain amid the squeal and crash of iron couplings and a frightening whoosh of steam. In this fantasy, she was tired and hopeful, with an old-fashioned suitcase in either hand, maybe a pillbox hat. She looked like Barbara Stanwyck. I was there to meet her in a wood-sided station wagon wearing a raincoat and galoshes and a fedora. Her mother seemed to be standing at the edge of this frame, tearfully waving a lace handkerchief goodbye, goodbye.

It was a scene out of black-and-white movies about idealistic screenwriters who planned to move to Hollywood, the Golden West, and make their fortune in the Promised Land and then send for the woman they loved. It would be hard at first, sure, but they were in love, they would make it, you bet.

What could I have been thinking? Could I have really been so desperate not to be alone that I imagined such an idea was even feasible? I was not a screenwriter, or even an idealist. Pittsburgh was not the Golden West, or the Promised Land. Were there any trains from Shreveport to Pittsburgh? If so, they surely weren't steam engines. And wasn't that guy in the dripping fedora George Raft?

And Traci was not the woman I loved. God forgive me, I knew this even at the time. I told her I loved her, sure, but come on. I hardly knew her. She was an okay writer for somebody her age, cute as all get-out, a willing sex partner. I appreciated all this. I was grateful, deeply grateful, I mean this sincerely. But really.

Let me be clear about this. Traci was a girl I had been sneaking around with on a university campus for a couple of months. That's who Traci was. A university is a place, maybe the only place on earth, where smart girls are deluded enough to think that a guy in a frayed corduroy coat and unpressed khakis would make a good life partner. And twice her age, don't forget about that. To her a salt-and-pepper beard and leather patches on the sleeves must have seemed good reasons to throw away your life and destroy your parents' dreams.

This was almost true but not quite. Traci had been young enough actually to consider seriously this ridiculous plan, this much was true. She thought it over, she applied her best college senior logic, she was adventurous, in the way of reckless youth, or post-traumatic stress disorder. I'm thinking of poor Jerry here. Not a bad plan, she must have thought. Not bad at all.

She would do it, she said. Honest to Pete she would, she really wanted to do it. She loved me and thought I was super and all, so it was definitely a good idea, throwing her life away. The thing was, though, she needed some, like, assurances.

Assurances, I said. Oh, right, assurances, you bet. Anything, I said, yes, of course, just name it, whatever you want, I could totally accommodate her, I was completely flexible, I only wanted her happiness. This was the way I talked. Sitting there on my library floor with these crinkly pages in my hands, it was all coming back to me.

We talked on the phone practically every day, her in Louisiana, me in Pittsburgh. Every conversation ended with me depressed and hopeless. I tried to stay positive, to plan ahead. I hoped to get a bed soon, for example. That was one goal. Possibly a chair.

I knew what I had to do, the diary said. I had to go to Shreveport. If I didn't go down to Louisiana to personally charm her, woo her, whatever—I'd be stuck in a new job in a new city with nothing at all to buffer me from my own sorry self. She would never go through with this if I didn't go fetch her personally.

I did it. I had no good excuse for abandoning my brand new classes, but that didn't matter. The airplane ticket would be expensive, I had little money, no credit card. That was okay too. I could come up with the cash for the plane ticket though not much more. None of this proved dissuasive. Shreveport here I come.

Traci met me at the airport. It was autumn in Pittsburgh but dead summer in Louisiana. The sun blazed down and sucked all the water out of the swamps. Great dark pools of malarial sweat appeared on my back and armpits and the seat of my pants. I might as well have been hacking sugar cane with a machete. Monkeys and bright birds seemed to screech from vines in Baggage. Jungle drums throbbed through the public address system. Alligators rolled over in the Avis rental booth. Or so it seemed to me, I swear.

Except that this Banana Republic representation is far too flattering. The corduroy and khaki and brush of beard that had seemed writerly and casual, even sexy, on a university campus, now in her hometown, looked like the steaming costume of a vagrant. Hobo Joe, riding the rails. I was wearing scuffed Hush Puppies. I looked like somebody who has been issued clothes at the shelter and is probably hiding a wine bottle in a paper bag.

Forget Traci's parents' ranch house with its picture window and 1950s sitcom smugness and central air, forget the yard full of towering loblolly pines and the riding mower parked under a nifty vinyl shed, and the blue blue kidney-shaped pool and pool furniture and umbrella in back of the house—her father was the successful manager of a chain of grocery stores—forget the gravel road in the middle of a swamp where this house stood, many miles from any city, beneath a dark cloud of mosquitoes as big as chicken hawks and loud as the string section of the Pittsburgh Symphony Orchestra—forget all this, though it is recalled in horror in my diary. They didn't live in Shreveport. They lived in an alternate universe. There were two suns in the brutal sky, just above the treetops. And yet something far more frightening than a time warp stood before me.

Traci's mother remains as the enduring memory of my arrival on this alien planet. I had felt her evil presence before. She had ridden with us in spirit in the car from the airport—

her handwritten instructions how to get to the airport from home, how to get back, what to do in case of an emergency (this was before widespread use of cell phones).

When we finally walked into the house and her mother saw me for the first time, she flinched like a child about to be slapped. This was the only time I felt almost sorry for her. I needed nothing more than that flinch to tell me what I looked like. My clothes, my beard, my age, my history, my sweaty crotch and armpits. I was foolish and vain and elderly. This is my reward, her mother might have said, for sacrificing to send my child to college.

Her mother, whose name is not recorded in either my diary or my memory, was a very thin, pinched-looking woman of about forty. Her lips were thin and tight and chapped. Her teeth were clenched. Her eyes were beads, and her expression was that of a person who has just smelled some odious thing, a fart, say, silent and deadly. Any latent impulse of mine to fantasize separate trysts with mother and daughter washed away like a spinning sinking dinghy on a flooded river. She managed to maintain this same unappealing visage throughout my visit, not merely as a first impression, though it is possible, in retrospect, that she was actually an attractive person, rendered monstrous by my repressed awareness that I was the monster not she.

Her father, also nameless these years later, was less threatening. He was a gentle-seeming, well-groomed little elf of a man with a tanned high forehead and ears that stuck out from his head. He wore brilliant white jogging shoes and baggy gabardine pants and a khaki shirt with the name of his grocery chain stitched above the pocket in red script. His face was open and profoundly sad, though he managed a wan smile on my account. I suppressed an impulse to hug him. I kept thinking that some funny slow-witted-sounding music ought to accompany him wherever he went. Dum dum de

112

dum boopy-de boopy-de boop. Something like that, like out of a cartoon about Baby Huey or Pluto or a nice duck.

When Traci introduced us—"Mommy, Daddy, this is my friend"—it was clear her mother was not going to make nice. She stood with her arms folded and looked away. She said nothing at all, but seemed momentarily to grow to an enormous size and become transformed to a fiery color and to grow horns and a tail. The diary says, "The house filled with the smell of sulfur." I don't think I was trying to be funny here. It is possible this moment reflects an LSD flashback from bad behavior some years earlier, but this is only conjecture and hard to pin down. The diary leaves this issue unsettled.

I extended my hand to Traci's father (whose name may have been Henry, come to think of it) and said, "I'm so glad to meet you."

He said, "How are you."

I said, "Fine, thanks, just fine, it's good to meet you."

He said, "How are you."

I understood then that mom and dad had agreed in advance to be civil to me—this much they owed their daughter, they must have allowed—but no more than that. They would be non-violent but not welcoming. My diary does not record whether this seemed fair to me at the time, though now it seems generous.

There is no need to record every scene of unpleasantness. At meals I made conversation I thought would be interesting, and they sat stone-faced and unresponsive. I told stories that I knew to be funny, and they looked at me as if I had spoken in Chinese. Eventually I started cutting stories short just to get to the end of them, with the result that the stories made no sense at all. They looked at me not with pity but with the repressed alarm one might feel in the presence of a madman, which is what I was, of course.

Traci was clearly embarrassed by me. She was irritated, angry with me. She wouldn't look at me when we were sitting together by the pool; she would suddenly leave a room without speaking and stay gone for long periods of time.

I became lonely and fearful. Then I became possessive. I started to follow Traci wherever she went. I asked her to go for a walk with me to a nearby pond. We walked there and tossed a few pebbles in the water. We heard a car and looked up. Her mother had thought we were gone too long and had come to get us. We piled in the back seat like first-graders.

Her father said, "Don't you know blacks drive up and down this road shooting pistols?"

Traci said, "Today, Daddy?"

He said, "No, not today, but they do it."

At times I thought things might be getting better. We had sex on the sofa when her parents were out of the house.

Traci said, "I guess we both needed that."

It was the first moment I had been happy since I arrived.

The respite was fleeting, though. Her mother's tight-lipped silence continued. The music continued to follow her father. Traci's distance from me slowly increased again.

By Thursday night—I had arrived in Louisiana on a Tuesday—Traci said, "My coming to Pittsburgh may not be such a great idea after all."

The hour was late, the night pitch black; her parents were already asleep; the mosquitoes outside were already carrying away small farm animals.

I said, "Okay, that's it, you don't love me, we're broken up, it's over, that's all, you had your chance."

I won't even try to analyze this. I'm just reporting what's in the diary.

She said, "Can't we at least talk about it?"

There was an argument, of course. We went through the usual clichés, accusations. "Don't tell me what I'm feeling," somebody said. "Your parents really did a number on you, didn't they," I managed to throw in. "Oh, so now you can read minds," she said. I even remembered to use a couple of expressions I had recently learned in therapy. "We are all responsible for our own pain," was one mentioned in my diary, though I can't say I knew what I was talking about. I think I just liked the way it sounded. The word "pain" dignified what was happening, somehow.

What I did know was that I suddenly felt better. This silly fight, with its hackneyed accusations, had touched something familiar and good in me. Dignity was a good word for what I felt. The more like soap opera this argument became, the more my spirits lifted. I felt not just better—I felt good. I felt wonderful, in fact. This argument was more life-affirming to me than anything I'd felt since I envisioned the 1940s-style reunion of lovers on the train platform. Better even than the sex earlier in the day. I don't mean I felt good because I was standing up for myself, either. This new life in me was not empowerment or self-respect or anything so lame or ephemeral.

This was melodrama. It is what had been missing. Melodrama gave life meaning. Melodrama made me whole again. Sleeping on the floor under an overcoat in Pittsburgh was not a low point, it was an ideal I had striven for and achieved. I loved sleeping on the floor beneath an overcoat. It made me feel young again. No, not young, dramatic, important. I felt like a writer. I was Henry Miller in Paris when I pulled that overcoat up to my chin and let my sock-feet hang out. This sweltering tropical night near the Gulf of Mexico I was Graham Greene, as we fought in our pajamas beneath a drone of mosquito wings. Someday I would write about this. I loved pain. Pain was my friend.

I flung away from Traci and reeled into the guest room which I had been assigned to. I may have even had the back of my hand to my forehead. I could hear Traci crying, possibly weeping. Yes, that girl was weeping, God bless her. I listened to her for a long time. She was a wonderful crier. Sobbing and snotty and gasping. This was nice, very nice, and I was grateful for her participation, but at last it was too much for me. I was berserk with pain, and not the kind I loved.

You can only tolerate so much of a good thing, even romance. I wanted her to marry me and run away. I wanted to beg her to take me back. I knew I could not. Not now. It was much too soon for that. And it had to be her idea. I would be breaking the rules of melodrama if I caved now. If I broke the rules, I would be left with nothing. I was not crazy enough to imagine that caving and begging would actually work anyway. The best I could do was to make her beg me not to leave. Or at least to give me a blowjob. I hoped she understood this. Otherwise, it was going to be a long night. I would say no, of course, but still.

I burst out of the guest room. I checked my reflection in the hall mirror. Not bad. Tragic, yes, handsome, yes. Not bad at all. Hobo Joe was nowhere to be seen.

"I can't stay," I declared. "I can't sleep in a house where no one loves me." What was I talking about? I hadn't slept in a house where anybody loved me for years.

"But I do love you," she wept.

This girl was good. She might as well have had a script. I didn't think this at the time, of course.

"It's no use," I said.

I packed my bag. Underwear, socks, shirts, toothbrush—I stuffed them in crazily, helter-skelter. We were speaking in stage whispers so as not to awake her parents.

I opened the front door and looked out into the night, down that long country road. I looked hopefully for a carload of blacks out shooting pistols. Maybe they would give me a ride to the bus station.

Traci threw her body in front of me to prevent me from walking into the darkness. "Threw her body, etc." are the actual words in my diary.

116

She said, "I won't let you go."

I said, "You must."

She said, "It's stupid. It's just stupid."

(This last line of dialogue I translated to "dangerous" or "insane" or some more acceptable word than "stupid.")

Finally I agreed to let her drive me to a bus station. As the nearest bus station was either Shreveport or Magnolia, Arkansas, thirty miles either way, I felt a good deal of relief not to be heading out on foot in the middle of the night. No telling when those guys with the pistols would have shown up.

We left notes to her parents on the kitchen table, in case they should wake up before Traci got back and wonder where we were, and eased out of the driveway.

I can cut this short. Nothing worked out. We drove to Magnolia. The bus station was closed until Saturday, for some reason, and I didn't have enough money for a bus ticket anyway. So we drove on back home. I stayed the weekend at Traci's house so I could get Super-Saver rates on my airline ticket. We got along pretty well and had sex one more time before I left for good, which was about the best anyone could have hoped for. It was just a bad plan all around. That's where I stopped reading the diary.

Annie came into the library and found me sitting on the floor looking at the yellowing pages. She had an armload of her mother's things, mostly framed pictures and old photograph albums. She plopped herself down on the floor beside me and let the albums spill off her lap.

I said, "This is a diary. From, you know, back in the day."

She said, "You don't talk like that," and we both laughed.

She said, "Look."

She opened one of her mother's albums that she had brought into the room. She turned each page, the first, the second, and so on to the end, pausing on each page before going on to the next. Then she put that album aside and did the same with the next. She showed me the picture frames, too, some with old photographs, some empty.

At first I wasn't sure what she was showing me.

Then I said, "She's removed all the pictures of herself as an old person."

There was Annie's mom as a child with her three sisters. There she was under a bower with some young man before a high school party of some kind. There she was in a group photo at Women's College standing beside a girl who would later become a world famous writer. There she was as a young mother in a polka-dot dress with baby Annie in her arms. All the spaces where her picture as an old woman had been were empty, bare and faded, where photographs had been removed. Traces of old glue still remained. We looked at a portrait of her as a slender bare-shouldered girl with a stylish 1920s haircut and a Mona Lisa smile.

Annie said, "This is how she wanted to be remembered. Not as an old woman."

We stood up finally. We gathered up the things we had been holding. Annie was sad for what she had lost, and I tried to comfort her. There was not much I could say. I loved her so much. I was an old fart, in love with his wife—that about summed it up for me—but it was a life I had chosen and a life I loved. No other would have been so good.

And so that is what happened the day I found an old diary as Annie cleaned out her late mother's belongings.

There is one more thing worth telling about the diary, I suppose. I looked back at it once more. Those notes Traci and I had written to her parents—I read that part of the entry.

My note said, "I hope that you'll understand that what we're doing tonight was done out of love and anguish, and has nothing to do with either of you." That's what I wrote. A suicide note. Or maybe a marriage announcement. How else

118

could such nonsense be interpreted? Melodrama had been the main nutrient in my emotional diet in those days. Why didn't I just say I'd decided to go back to Pittsburgh early? Why didn't I say Traci was driving me to the bus station? And yet, sitting on the floor of my well-appointed library, in the shadow of my good books and rich paintings, I hungered again for that heavenly food. I wanted to be that impulsive, melodramatic, desperate person again. I held Annie's mother's albums, with the missing snapshots, and cried for what was lost, with no thought of what was gained. I looked again at the diary.

On the way back home from the closed bus station, Traci and I realized how our note sounded. We sped into the driveway and set the brake. We scrambled out of the car giggling like middle-schoolers and found the notes where we left them. Nobody had waked up. No harm was done. We were exhausted. We went to our separate beds. The mosquitoes were nesting in the tree limbs like buzzards.

Rob Griffith

33: For My Wife's Birthday

Your birthday's come around again, and I
can think of nothing but those 33s
collecting dust behind the stairs. Fading,
their cardboard jackets hold a thousand ghosts—
the brooding bands, standing with arms crossed
in front of brick walls or railroad tracks
that needle-off to infinity; moonscapes
in psychedelic reds, blues, and black;
the denim jackets, the moussed hair, the scowls,
the desert landscapes. They wait in the silence cast
by all the years. And I wish I could rise
above the clouds, above this disc of stars
and dust, and gently lift the needle up
and back. I'd let it slip into the groove,
that first song yawning out a sunrise,
the vinyl night spinning down to nothing.
And every time, before that last track ends,
I'd lift the needle yet again, content
to hear these same old songs, desperate
to avoid the hiss before it plays, or after.

STEVE YATES

from Coin of the Realm
(Or: A Local Student Recognizes How Jim
Whitehead Can Inhabit Any Character Who
Is Large and Radiates Mysterious Force)

The first time lawyer Ducat was called upon to serve his town
of Port Gibson, Mississippi, a newly elected administration
was gearing up in Washington and all over the empire people
were in a fervor, especially Ducat's law partner, Priester. As
soon as the steam whistle at the cottonseed oil mill hooted its
call to work, heard all across the town, Priester lit in.

The partners were on speaking terms that week in July of
2001 because both had recorded billable hours from paying
clients. Availing himself of this détente, Priester expanded
on his satisfaction with the return to morality and the end
to lies and subterfuge in government. A portly man with a
balding head that retained a neatly trimmed ring of sparkling
black hair above his ears, he paced as he extolled the new
regime and its rectitude.

Ducat, a Catholic, tolerated his born-again Baptist
colleague's enthusiasm. After all, Ducat had voted for the
new president as well. But he thought this gassing about
the moral high ground was a lot of tedious bullshit. And he
was about to say so after enduring the first hour of it when,
mercifully, in walked Sterling Estep, Port Gibson's official
city attorney and the most venerated lawyer in Claiborne
County.

The restored Frisson Building, now the offices of Ducat
& Priester, was once a general store. Its interior first floor
remained open and high-ceilinged with hammered copper
looming greenly above filigreed iron columns and a refinished
hardwood floor. Without partitions and without the finances

to keep a receptionist, both partners in competition greeted prospective clients and all-comers.

"Why, Sterling Estep, Hotty Toddy," Priester offered, a welcome Ducat could not match, having graduated from Washington University Law School in St. Louis rather than the predominant Ole Miss.

Estep, a bear of a man with wavy silver hair and blue eyes, grunted at Priester and raised a large hand in a wave that both dispensed a show of recognition and dismissed his junior. "Ducat," Estep said.

Ducat gestured to the Frisson's old counting pen, now the law office's conference room and the only place where privacy could be maintained. Estep followed him. With a smirk at the crestfallen Priester, Ducat shut the counting room door behind them.

Estep stretched his tremendous arms at his waist, shaking the cuffs of his seersucker coat into place. His face, white skin flecked with gin blossoms along his cheeks, was reddened from walking in the July swelter. In his hair sweat darkened some of his silver to iron gray. He dabbed his forehead with a handkerchief, not embroidered, and it pleased Ducat that Estep, who could afford ostentation, chose to be practical.

Ducat offered him ice water and a seat at the antique library table. Estep took the glass but not the chair. "Not ready to sit," he said. And so they stood.

"You see, Ducat, it's this way," Estep began. Then he said nothing for such a long time Ducat worried that he had missed something obvious. "I'm not getting any younger."

Ducat held his tongue knowing Estep brooked no compliments.

Estep pulled out a brass money clip, peeled off ten one-hundred-dollar bills, and laid them on the table. "That's retainer. Take it, nothing leaves this room."

Ducat left the bills alone. "Tell me what's the matter."

122

Estep lost his preoccupied air. With his blue eyes widening he gave Ducat a reassessment from head to toe. Ducat sensed the adrenaline of the courtroom ache warmly along his waistline.

"All right, then. Something in the wind about the cottonseed oil mill. ADM maybe has had enough."

Ten years ago Archer-Daniels Midland had purchased the seed oil plant, the largest employer in town, from the family owners, one of whom Ducat represented facing off against Estep, who represented the majority shareholder.

"What are your sources?" Ducat asked.

Estep pressed two fingers to the bills and, with the considered care of large men, nudged them forward.

Not without some hesitation, Ducat turned his back on Estep and made to pour himself a glass from the pitcher dripping with condensation. "Counselor, it was your client who picked off the enfeebled and less secure of his own kin to accumulate a majority and force a sale." Ducat drew out the process of pouring so that each ice cube clattered down. The counting pen held an odd shape, a narrow rectangle that lost some of its ceiling at one end to the triangular jut of the staircase above it. This jut sometimes made the room feel close, as it did now.

Over his shoulder Ducat heard Estep breathing, rough and hard. The fabric of Estep's suit rustled; a joint cracked. Ducat imagined the giant tensing, clenching his fists. But when he turned, he found Estep collapsed in a chair as if he had been blown back by a cyclone, one leg flung out, one hand gripping his face.

Ducat leaned a hip on the library table, sipped his water, and watched Estep, a scalding and guilty pleasure filling him. Ducat was a tall man, though not as tall as Estep, svelte, with a full head of brownish-red hair he kept in a cut as close as a National Guardsman might. He often wore leather suspenders to accentuate his height and leanness, and he sported a black bow-tie today, knotted so securely it seemed the ebony handle to a pressure valve rather than an article of clothing.

"Port Gibson," Estep said, "cannot lose that mill." Slowly and dramatically he drew his hand down his face, leaving gray streaks in the red of his skin. His eyes narrowed. "Ducat," he said. "Help me."

With deliberate slowness Ducat set his glass down on a coaster. Then he took the ten one-hundred-dollar bills, folded and slipped them into the pocket of his slacks. He sat down across from Estep. "What do you know?"

In its latest corporate report ADM outlined several areas pressuring revenue growth, chief among them cottonseed oil, which now faced competition from more economically refined vegetable oils. While intrigued that Estep might be a direct investor in ADM or might have received shares in lieu of payment, Ducat also understood how to read the future in hints from a prospectus.

And, Estep told him, an ADM Chief Financial Officer with an entourage of assistants had just finished a stay at the Grand Gulf Inn outside of town. "High level attention. Hasn't happened like this since they bought."

Ducat smoothed the crease in his trousers. "Is there more?"

"Two extra managers brought down from Illinois. Haven't bought homes. Staying with the plant superintendent. Whole month now."

Ducat said nothing and waited long enough that doubt and anger crept across Estep's broad, handsome face. He was glad he could torture Estep a little: Estep had been beyond a zealous advocate when the sale was at stake. With no court or jury to bring decorum, the negotiations combined both bad theater and a tavern brawl. Ten years younger then but still massive and athletic, Estep thrived in such a melee, frightening even the ADM lawyers from Illinois and New

124

York. Estep's performance, though, was needless—his client held the majority. It could have all been transacted with icy courtesy. But Estep chose always to do things unforgettably. Now this mess.

"In what way," Ducat asked once he had Estep boiling, "is this issue ripe?"

Estep edged forward in his chair and loomed in on Ducat. His voice was a whisper. "That's it. That's why I want you with me, Ducat. You don't fuck around. You get it."

Ducat did not move an inch, though his heart was pounding. Despite the seersucker and French cuffs, there was no avoiding it: being this close to such a behemoth poised at the edge of his chair. It was as if Ducat were facing a linebacker crouched ready in his final stance. "I am afraid in this case I do not get it. What you have outlined are certainly troubling indications." Ducat paused. "But the mill belongs to ADM, as does the initiative and any potency."

Estep breathed deeply and leaned back slowly. He regarded Ducat with a relaxed smile. "Now you're with me," he said. He let loose a roaring laugh. "Together!" He clapped Ducat on the shoulder with stupefying force. "Onward!" Estep stood.

And, though nonplussed, so did Ducat. Estep turned to the door, and Ducat, groping to understand just what exactly had concluded, opened the door to the counting pen and ushered Estep out. Without a glance back, without even so much as a grunt to the expectantly rising Priester, Estep surged across the lobby and slammed the Frisson's glass door behind him. The finely stenciled name of Ducat & Priester, PC seemed to quiver.

After a moment, Ducat sat at his desk blinking. The cottony parchment of the thousand dollars in his pocket shifted crisply and he smoothed the outline of the bills through his slacks. Then in his leather-bound log he recorded the retainer and, with much struggle, an abstract of the discussion.

"Well?" Priester asked after several minutes of venomously watching him. "What was that all about?"

Ducat continued to write and did not look up. "I am under retainer, counselor, if you don't mind, please."

"St. Louis," Priester spat.

Then all talk between them was at an end.

W. D. Blackmon

from Ruby

Claire and I are waiting patiently at the bathroom door when it mysteriously creaks open. Instinctively, I'm turning Claire in the other direction and getting ready to hide Claire's eyes, and I guess that's a good thing. What I see is uncanny. Jill's ninety-year-old grandfather is hunched down over the rust-stained toilet, his arms braced around the top of the bowl, his head dipped inside, vigorously lapping up the water. He doesn't notice us at first, but I startle him, I guess, in my effort to shift Claire around. He looks at me with the heaviest kind of grief I've ever seen. Like he's finally been found out, like he's the first person in the history of the world to actually watch his soul slip away before his eyes. Water is dripping in delicate streams down his chin in the shadowy room. His skin is pale and splotched, and seems very close against his skull. There's a big blue vein standing out on his temple like a well-defined river system on a map. Clearly, I don't know how to break the ice here, but something needs to be said. Claire is squirming and craning her neck. She says, "Why him down there, Daddy?"

I say, "Claire, this is your great-grandfather—your Grandma Ruth's dad. You remember your grandaddy, don't you?" To him, I say, "This is Claire, your granddaughter. She has to go pee-pee really bad." I put down Claire, who is tugging fiercely not to be put down and tell her, "Your granddad needs some help here," which relaxes her grip enough for me to put her down. I grab him under the armpits and say, "I'm going to help lift you up. If you *want* to get up, that is."

He does, it seems, but he mainly just stands up himself now that he's ready. He's still a really strong old man--you'd have to be to drink very long in that position. When he's upright, he seems OK. With a weird vacant look, he says wistfully, "Thirsty . . . mighty thirsty . . . I felt kinda funny . . . weak . . . ." I take out one of the paper towels I always keep in my pockets for the kids and gently wipe off his chin.

Soon I'm shuffling along with him toward the front door, holding his hand in one hand and Claire's in the other. As we pass the big stove, he seems to get a little cocky and says, "You wouldn't happen to have a little whiskey on you, would you?" and grins at his joke, like he knows it's funny and not acceptable in this situation to ask that (some of his children out there would tell you it would be better for you to drink hydrochloric acid than take a sip of whiskey), and its being so unacceptable is what's so funny about it, but you can tell he *would* like some whiskey.

I say, "No, I don't have any whiskey on me. I wish I did. If I find any, I'll let you know."

When we get to the front door of the schoolhouse, he surveys out the screen at the panorama of beautiful people he has begotten (or that his children or grandchildren have). Finally, he says, "Who are these people?"

I answer, "They're all yours. They're all here because of you. You—"

He interrupts my version of the genesis of the Hawkinses and says, "I feel like I know these people. There sure are some good lookin' kids out there."

I say, "I know it. There sure are. Now, we better sit you down on this porch. There's Nancy over there, and there's Margaret (both his daughters). Lunch is going to be ready any minute." Claire is patting the old slat-bottomed chair on the front porch where we're trying to get him to sit down. Eight-year-old Andrew runs by us heading for the toilet. "Claire, here," I say to him, "has to go pee-pee *really* bad, so

128

we've gotta go." That does the trick, and he sits down while we head off to one of the outhouses at the back corners of the yard behind the schoolhouse, the nearest one about eighty feet away in the sun, which is blazing away now out from behind a huge bank of ultra-white clouds. Shafts of light are slanting out from behind the clouds. When I was little, I always associated this with the immediate presence of God.

We're on our way over the dusty, dry grass, and occasional flint-like rock poking up out of the ground. We're heading down the slope toward the outhouse, picking up speed. There is a big drop-off behind the back fence just behind both outhouses, and the drop-off opens into a picturesque vista of steep oak-and-hickory-and-walnut-and-sassafras-covered hills. Claire asks, "What him doing on the bathroom floor?"

I start to lie and say something like, "Well, he was just cleaning the toilet . . ." but think better of it. I simply say, "He's your granddad. He's very old. He doesn't always know what he's doing. I'll tell you what he was doing if you won't be worried." Claire promises not to be worried, and, somehow, after doing that, she never is (less than a year ago she was morbidly worried about the physical well being of the whole natural world, hysterically taking to heart the death or injury of every insect and bird or of anyone she ever heard of in conversation or on TV—screaming hysterically when she saw a man stabbed in the back on *Spartacus*—we had even forgotten the TV was on). Somehow, now, this promising not to be worried lets her take the parent's role. She assumes I'm the one who'll be hysterical and worried (which is true, actually), and now she always reassures me with a tender and loving condescension. "Claire," I say, "he was taking a drink in the toilet. But don't you ever take a drink like that. He didn't know what he was doing. There has been poo-poo and pee-pee in that water, and the pee-pee and poo-poo germs could make you very sick. But I think he'll be OK . . . . Oh, and, Claire, promise me you won't tell anyone about your granddad's drinking like that. That would make him very sad." Getting down all the fine print on Claire's promises not to drink from toilets, or puddles, or bathwater, or birdbaths, or things like that and not to tell about her grandfather today takes most of the trip to the outhouse. But before we get to the outhouse it strikes me that Rachael must surely have abandoned Ruby by now and that Ruby is probably lying on the filthy old cookhouse floor, crying and ingesting lead paint flakes and rat feces and inhaling and absorbing in any and every way possible every conceivable kind of pesticide and insecticide and awful old cleaning agent. And then it strikes me that it will soon be lunch time, and Jill and I will have to rig up some system of feeding Ruby and Claire with the minimum amount of danger, mess, and trauma.

There seem to be so many mountainous troubles immediately confronting me and ranged interminably one behind the other as far as I can imagine I feel a weight miraculously float off my shoulders. All together it's too much to worry about, so I don't worry about any of it. Reaching for the slick gray wooden handle of the outhouse door, I say, "Well, Claire, it looks like we've gone from the penthouse to the outhouse." Opening the door and stepping inside, Claire and I hit an overwhelming stench and heat. But, somehow, once we're inside and shut the door, we're a part of it and it's not so bad. I'm busy tracking all the buzzing wasps and suspended spiders inside and keeping the flies off Claire and getting her ready to go pee-pee. Claire, good-naturedly seated on the wooden hole, says, "I going to go pee-pee *and* poo-poo," and I know we're in for a twenty- or thirty-minute siege. Claire is some kind of prodigy when it comes to poo-poo. She's like a poo-pooing lumberjack in the body of a thirty-pound little girl. So, knowing it's pee-pee *and* poo-poo now, I'm content to sit and talk to her and wait—or I would be if it weren't for Ruby surely abandoned in the cookhouse. But I have to resign myself now; there's just no getting back to her for awhile.

I talk to Claire about the spiders, wasps, and flies, and tell her we'll keep track of them, and she'll be OK. What I don't tell her is that there might be a copperhead coiled up under the seat she's on. But I'm almost psychedelically tuned in to any danger to her. There's a fat rust-colored red wasp crawling nosily up the weathered wood about a foot from the side of Claire's head, but she doesn't see it. There's a suspicious black spider in a web up in one corner. Claire's watching a Granddaddy Longlegs spider crawl up the inside of the outhouse door. She says, "I don't like that 'sfider."

I tell her, "Well, Little Miss Muffet, it doesn't like you, either, but it's totally harmless. You better just relax; this is where all these bugs live. We're in their house."

She says, "This them house? Where them mom?"

I answer, "That spider is called a Granddaddy Longlegs—kind of like *your* granddaddy—your great-granddaddy—with his long legs, right? But maybe that *is* the mom. Maybe it's the kid. Maybe it's the daddy. Once she thinks of insects or animals as moms, dads, or kids, she has trouble attributing any evil motive to them.

Sitting out in the stink and still shadows of the outhouse, something triggers a flash of the dream I had last night and first remembered beginning driving to Valley Spring earlier this morning, which, I guess, is why I can still remember it. I'm the Assistant District Attorney, and the gentle, funny, scholarly older lawyer who is my boss is named Richard Beckett. Well, this dream was full of totally unbearable tension, anxiety, depression, and mystery, and set amidst the backdrop of absolutely crucial international intrigue (my inheritance from television). I, of course, had to succeed at some Kafkaesque challenge I didn't even really understand,

and the fate of the world hinged on my performance. The arch villain of the dream was none other than Richard Beckett, but not the mild-mannered and aristocratically ironic Richard Beckett I knew as a colleague but one who was ruthless and sadistic, a skilled assassin with a hunting bow with a telescopic sight. He had stalked me in a high-rise parking garage and hit me in the thigh from a seemingly impossible angle and distance. As I dragged my leg along pathetically, trying to get to the elevator in time to escape the next and surely fatal arrow, he yelled from several floors above, "You have just begun to taste the vengeance of the Reba McIntyre Brigade!" And sometime in the night, the militaristic flavor continuing, I had this dream of the Nazis parachuting horses ridden by neatly-dressed SS officers into Paris. At the time, I kept thinking, "They make it look so easy!" I suppose if the Nazis ever joined forces with the Reba McIntyre Brigade and the Christian rock stars, they could conquer the world. Of course, in the Memorial Day sunlight, these dreams seem pretty silly, but, still there's a tinge of that creepy, ominous feeling I felt dreaming them left over, and I keep thinking that if I could recapture my dreams completely enough and find those missing ingredients that evaporate upon waking, I'd be well on my way to discovering the secret of life.

Claire is still in the middle of her epic poo-poo adventures. Usually, we just talk until she's done, however long that takes. Now, however, she seems self-absorbed, making satisfied little popping noises with her lips. If Claire is going poo-poo like this, her legs go to sleep because the circulation is cut off, with all her weight resting on a little part of her thighs and her feet dangling in the air. So, I'm absent-mindedly lifting her legs now and then and watching for potentially dangerous and irritating insects. About every forty-five seconds, I get a prickle of panic about Ruby being left alone in the cookhouse. I know there are a hundred and something people around, with probably ten or twenty in the cookhouse around noon-time. And, besides, Rachael's supposed to be watching her, but it seems like the most disastrous and careless thing I've ever done to leave her like this.

Lately I've been having these weird thoughts that giving Ruby the name Ruby was some kind of jinx. I thought of that name because of that old Rolling Stones' song "Ruby Tuesday" that I heard as a kid, but now a franchise restaurant named Ruby Tuesday's has moved into town, and I feel like I might as well have named her Cheddar's or T.G.I. Friday's or Applebee's. And every association with the name I run into lately has a crummy connotation—even the biblical reference seems not quite thought out, "A good woman is more valuable than rubies." Isn't that how it goes? Well, *how many* rubies? If she is worth her weight in rubies, then that would be something like $227,000,000.00 for a hundred-pound woman. Then there's Jack Ruby, Ruby Begonia, and Ruby Ridge. And the grocery store Muzac oldies song, "Ruby, Ruby, Ruby . . . when will *you be* mine?" The very worst, of course, is Kenny Rogers' old song, "Ruby," in which the crippled Viet Nam vet pleads mentally to his wife, "Ruby, don't take your love to town," and then thinks that if he were less crippled, he'd "put 'er in the ground." Why not just divorce Ruby and mentally seethe about putting Lyndon Johnson or Richard Nixon in the ground? This vet suffers the perfect Country Western self-pitying producing torture. He's a quadriplegic with great hearing and a cheatin' wife.

The part I always remembered from the Rolling Stones' song was, "Goodbye, Ruby Tuesday . . . who could hang a name on you? When you change with every new day, still I'm going to miss you . . ." with this really exotic twang that echoed off into infinity at that point. That part seems kind of mysterious and wistful to me, even now, but lately I heard the whole song on the oldies' channel, and it gave me the chills. The line that got me the most was, "Lose your dreams, and you will lose your mind." Well that whole section went, "Dying all the time / Lose your dreams, and you will lose your mind / In life unkind." There's really an ugly bump in the rhythm at the end with that "In life unkind." I thought parts of the song were ugly and stupid, and I was astounded I'd named my child after such a song. Hearing the song like that just gave me the creeps connecting it all to my Ruby.

One weird game in perspective I play to raise Ruby up is that I'm always looking for angles that show how people who seemingly have it made actually are more ridiculous or pathetic than they appear—as if that will give Ruby a little boost, as one of the absolute majority of troubled and stricken and absurd people in the world. For example, I'll see Catherine Callaway on the CNN news late at night and notice that I can see up her nostrils (a little ways, anyway)—an unexpected disadvantage for the turned-up Barbie-type nose. So, I argue in Ruby's behalf, *anyone* can appear at a disadvantage. As I gloat, connecting Ruby and Catherine Callaway in the same plight, suddenly I notice that—after prolonged observation—Catherine, her nose holes pointed proudly toward the camera—doesn't look so bad that way, after all. In fact, she starts to look very good. She has on a fairly high fashion version of an old double-breasted men's suit, but she doesn't have a blouse on. The wide lapels only partially cover her breasts. She is totally articulate and ravishing and she has a great job and her nostrils are absolutely wonderful. Twist and turn it any way I want, it doesn't seem that Catherine Callaway started out life hit in the head with a sledgehammer . . . although maybe her nostrils were monkeyed around with just a little bit.

I've heard that if a couple has a child die, the odds are strong that they'll break up soon and get divorced. I keep wondering if Jill and I are in that category. Obviously, Ruby hasn't died, but it's like we're holding our breath waiting for her to be born. Jill works so hard with her, hour after hour, day after day, and gets more and more often into a deep depression over it all. I tend to get mad defending Ruby, saying the worse off she is, the more she needs our help, not us moping around—which is hardly fair, since Jill does most of the work, and I guess you can't really control lying wide-eyed awake all night because your baby is brain-injured and there's nothing on earth you can do about it. A few weeks ago, we were having a terrible fight about this—in front of Claire, to make things worse—and Jill said, tears streaming down her face, "She's my baby, and I'll cry if I want to." Jill and I started laughing uncontrollably, and Claire started laughing because we were laughing, and then it took about thirty minutes for me to explain to Claire why we were laughing, the allusion to the old song, "It's my party, and I'll cry if I want to . . . ," etc.

Every one-year-old I see is like a raving genius, an affront to Ruby, somehow. They're starting to walk and talk, they can pick up a ball, they can recognize their parents and light up when they see them, they can see food on the table and recognize it as food and know that they're hungry. Sometimes I just wince and turn away. I want them to be happy. I want them to be normal. It's not jealousy, in the usual sense; I just feel so protective of Ruby sometimes I can't bear to watch. At our visit to the Genetics Clinic I saw Down's kids Ruby's age tumbling around and hanging off the ledge of the reception office window, and I envied that (they all seemed like Nadia Comaneci compared to Ruby). I see bumper stickers that proclaim, "Proud Parents of a Highland Jr. High Honor Student!" And I think about getting a bumper sticker that reads: "Proud Parents of a Brain-Damaged Child!" But the funny thing is, I *am* proud of Ruby. I keep waiting for the first insult to come so I can totally destroy the person who dares insult her. I work out vengeful scenario after vengeful scenario, centered around the most thoughtless people I know. But everyone is always totally thoughtful and understanding. At home I'm sure they feel relieved they've been spared such trouble—and that's natural. What they don't realize is that Jill and I aren't the ones with the burden—not really—Ruby is. And there's the sticking point for me; I just can't ever work my mind around it. I really don't feel sorry for myself; I feel sorry for Ruby.

Right at the peak of my self-pitying introspection, Claire says, "I done." It strikes me that I'm glad I don't have much time to think about our troubles lately. I lift Claire off the wooden circle and fish out the paper towel I wiped off her great-granddad's chin with. I work away cleaning Claire and wish I had some baby wipes. "Claire," I say, struggling to get her clean without hurting her, "you are one poo-pooing girl."

Laughing, she pulls her dress up even higher and says, "Kidnap, Daddy! I going be kidnap!" This is one of her latest jokes. She heard the mom of a four-year-old cousin say a few days ago, "Jennifer, if you don't put your swimming suit back on, you're going to be kidnapped!" So Claire has started thinking that any time she's naked and can be seen she runs a good risk of being kidnapped. She makes kidnapping seem like a lot of fun. She asked me what it was, so I told her, trying not to worry her too much—saying that there really wasn't much kidnapping in our area, especially in our neighborhood, and we wouldn't let her be kidnapped, even if there were. But, I said, there were some "mean men" around (she's sexist with her idea about mean *men*, but rightly so, I guess), and although we would never let mean men hurt her, she had to be careful—without worrying too much (of course, she asked how much *was* too much). That's what I said, but what I thought about was the TV show Jill saw that included an interview with a man in prison who kidnapped and killed little girls and boys Claire's age. He took pictures of the process along the way, keeping a photo album, with the last photo in each series being the body of the child hung on a hook in his closet. Before he began killing each new child, he showed her or him the photo album of the previous victims so that they realized that was about to happen to them.

Wigger

Over a span of weeks in the fall of 1995, Cal Ripken, Jr. broke Lou Gehrig's consecutive games streak and Michael Jordan began his first season following his initial retirement. During that same stretch, I started my first semester at Northern Missouri, a small liberal arts college where I was set to play NAIA basketball. By the time fall practice rolled around, twice a day, with sessions in the weight-room and on the track, those feel-good stories from the world of sports came in handy. I tacked *Sports Illustrated* covers on my walls, reminding myself why I was going through this hell, months away from my anticipated glory of the regular season. At the very least, I needed to keep ingrained in myself the mottos that push us to sweat, push us to continue, push us to buy tennis shoes. Eventually, though, a story that had begun over a year earlier within the world of sports, and had then spilled over into the World itself, hogged all the media attention, defined by a single moment in early October.

Justice was being served in California.

Morning conditioning drills and a biology exam had wiped me out, and I crashed restlessly on my top bunk the sticky afternoon O.J. was acquitted of thwapping the heads off his ex-wife and a Hollywood waiter. My roommate, Hubert, engrossed by the action on CNN, considered waking me when the jurors strolled back into the L.A. courtroom, but he decided against it. Hubert was also a freshman, and as a member of the junior varsity, he was required to practice only once a day. His laziness often left him as tired as I was, and I don't believe he wanted to waste the energy it would've taken to stand from the couch, make a 180° turn, and shake my 230 pound frame conscious.

He needn't have worried, though. Within seconds of the not-guilty verdict, the third story of Maddox Hall, a three-story dormitory erected in the sixties (and, other than the brilliant J.D. Burns Athletic Complex, the newest building on Northern Missouri's square block of land), flickered briefly, then ruptured to life, fellow freshmen and sophomores rushing from door-to-door, most of them grinning, both confounded and elated, yelling, "Did you see that?" and, "He got off, baby!" The shaved-headed white guy who lived next door stopped by to repeat the news we heard echoing in the hallways. He ambled with a fake limp and spoke like a gangsta rapper. Hubert and I called him G-Funk.

"Word," he said. "Boy didn't do it!"

I yawned, and uncovered. The residence halls weren't air conditioned, and I peeled off my shirt, sitting up on my bed, Indian-style, in only my underwear. This minimal fashion was common for many Maddox residents, shaken by the exile from their parents' air-conditioned homes.

Hubert said, "Thanks for the update, G-Funk."

"Second floor was gonna go mad crazy if that jury'd ruled him guilty," he told us.

While the third floor of Maddox consisted primarily of the white members and former members of the junior varsity and freshman basketball teams, more vocal with their celebrations, the second floor housed the black members of the junior varsity football and baseball teams. They were more subdued at this point. The white guys who celebrated, I figured, either felt some bogus connection to black culture, seeing as they'd grown up playing a sport heavily influenced by it—G-Funk was the strongest, most swaggering example of this—or they were spiteful and afraid of black culture, probably from what they'd seen during that culture's other recent spillage into the mainstream, the Rodney King riots, and they were happy they weren't going to get their heads caved in like academic Reginald Dennys. As for the second floor and the other residence hall, which was spooky and dilapidated, built well before the civil rights movement and predominantly black, their victory probably seemed tainted—a sell-out nigger that got away with something, instead of a born suspect who'd earned the gift of a fair trial.

"They were 'gonna go crazy,' G-Funk?" Hubert asked.

"Maybe riot," he said. "I was down for that."

"They were going to riot for O.J.?"

"But not now."

"Wow," I chuckled. "A race riot?"

"Hell, yeah."

Hubert said, "And what if O.J. would've actually been innocent?"

G-Funk didn't follow, but Hubert had already lost interest, flipping through the channels until he found a station that wasn't showing The Juice squeezing out tears of joy.

"You always been a big O.J. fan, G-Funk?" I pressed further. "He up there with Malcolm? 2Pac? Maybe the Fresh Prince?"

G-Funk pushed out his lips the way he pushed them when he tried to make them bigger, smirking, and said, "Fuck the Fresh Prince, man." He said, "Ha."

"Sell out bitch," Hubert agreed. "And fuck Carlton, too."

G-Funk chuckled in concurrence.

"Punk motherfucker," I threw in for good measure, able to talk that talk too, owning my fair share of Ice Cube CDs and several hood movies on VHS. Next to my *Sports Illustrated* covers were the theatrical poster for *Menace II Society* and an oversized Nike ad of a bald-headed Latrell Sprewell. Actually, I'd arrived at Northern Missouri cut from much of the same cloth that G-Funk stood cloaked in. The boredom of my small-town teenage years coincided nicely with rap music staking claim to the mainstream and the NBA becoming the most influential sport in America. Soon, television profiles on rich, urban twenty-somethings increased, and Foot Lockers throughout the country were filled with black socks, shorts like hoop skirts, and stylish sweatshirts emboldened with an embroidered continent of Africa and the word "Unity." My rebellious nature had a hand, too, and one of the better ways to rebel among my white, middle-class, Midwestern peers was to embrace the blossoming yet still dangerous Hip-Hop culture. (Ironically, this kind of rebellion would be futile with today's middle-class youth. As with all products, black culture has become a homogenized, non-toxic trend. One of the few ways kids can rebel these days is to open fire on their classmates or join the Taliban.)

Luckily, throughout my high school years, I always retained a fair amount of self-awareness concerning my Wigger reinvention, a combination of insecurity and restraint keeping me out of embarrassing situations—this is to say, if I made a journey out of suburbia, and encountered any actual black folks in the wild, I kept my Black-cent toned down and nudged my crooked baseball cap bill straight. Or, if I crooned along with a rap song laden with the word "nigga," I censored myself, substituting a caesura for the controversial utterance. This charade became clearest to me upon my arrival to Northern Missouri, surrounded by chumps who, for one reason or another, had created Wigger personas, as well. G-Funk and several guys like him seemed to lack discernment with their acts, though, often pushing the boundaries around the guys they'd lifted identities from in the first place. I was embarrassed for them when I wasn't one of them.

Now G-Funk asked me how practice was going and I shrugged, then climbed off the top bunk and took a Gatorade from our mini-fridge. In honor of our guest, I cranked up the most recent Snoop Dogg CD, as Hubert had given up on channel surfing.

"Word," G-Funk said, feeling out the beat with his shoulders.

I was too sore to jive along.

"This one," I told him, "is for O.J."

Snoop Dogg jawed of white bitches and Hennessy.

While I never lost my fascination with black people, varsity basketball hardly gave me a chance to keep up a façade. Being one of three white guys on a twelve-man squad expunged the need to play the role of the minority anyhow. Eight of the nine black guys on the team were from an area in Louisiana dubbed "The Boot," and Dennis Mouton called Texas home. Two of them were thirty years old. Our coach, Tom Piper, had a reputation for putting together collections of guys who'd eschewed opportunities for hard knock life-experience. Dennis, our center, fought in the Persian Gulf War. He graduated high school when I was in fifth grade. Sherman Rutherford had more tattoos on his body than I had chest and pubic hair. There were seven fathers on the team, and Koby would become a father during a debauched trip to New Orleans for a Thanksgiving tournament. Our locker room had more pictures of children than a hair salon.

NAIA basketball features more than 300 teams in 27 conferences, and is full of teams like ours, rich with colorful personalities who had NCAA Division I talent but missed out because of grades, attitudes, or the totally bizarre. Vance Wilson, our other thirty-year-old, had actually signed on with Syracuse University, a D-I power, fresh out of high school, but his tenure ended after a night in jail for assaulting someone he claims was a transsexual. (He always pointed out a wicked scar on his hip as proof that this transsexual was also a biter.) At this time, NAIA wasn't policed as stringently as NCAA

Division I, but winning was just as important to coaches and administrators who want to ascend in the coaching and administrating ranks. This led to practices that pushed the fringes of ethics, and Northern Missouri was notorious for riding those fringes, a veritable Statue of Liberty for the hard cases of college athletics—"Bring us your low grades, bring us your felonies, bring us your raw skill." Occasionally, an overachieving player slipped through the cracks—this was the case for me, my strength in the post and hustle, as well as Arnathan's looming suspension for non-existent grades, making up for my lack of natural talent, and paving my way to the varsity within days of my arrival on campus. Most of my fellow freshmen weren't so lucky.

During my time there, Northern Missouri ran a scam with tuition costs, based on the theory that people are suckers when they think they're getting a deal. No parents in their right minds would send their children to a college with resources as depleted as Northern Missouri's if they were paying four or five thousand dollars a year. But when these parents believed they were netting an eighteen thousand dollar a year education, which was Northern Missouri's list price, for a mere four thousand dollars, they lost rationality. Every year, Northern "recruited" kids from all around the area, promising them careers in orange and purple jerseys. While most of these kids had some talent, perhaps leading their tiny high schools to regional glory, they didn't have the talent it takes to compete at the college level. Many were undersized, adding to the lure of a dream they never thought possible. Proud parents fell for the ruse, too, believing their child had earned a discounted education and the right to play college basketball. The parents were informed, correctly, that NAIA schools can't offer full scholarships, but a partial basketball scholarship and a work-study program would cut into the tuition costs significantly. Meanwhile, their kids received basically the same deal that all the other students received under the guise of academic scholarships and grants.

Northern basketball brought in over sixty freshmen a year with this scam, fifteen of them making the junior varsity, fifteen making the freshman squad, and thirty or more regulated to a sort of second-class red-shirt status. These red-shirts weren't allowed to practice with the team. They were told to work on their skills (on their own time) and given a pat on the back that really meant "better luck next year." It wasn't much better for the freshman and junior varsity teams. They had to purchase their own jerseys and warm-ups, and were often relegated to playing games versus local AAU squads and military academies. The school took their money all the same, and a healthy portion was then channeled back to our varsity program.

These extra funds helped pay for our great uniforms, travel budget, and much of our tuition and living expenses. It paid for two pairs of shoes a season from a local dealer. We were also given the benefits of the work-study program in the form of monthly checks, but while the junior varsity and freshmen had to work cafeteria or custodial jobs with the rest of the student body, the members of the varsity worked ten hours a week for Coach Piper. My first semester at Northern, this job amounted to taking tickets at the volleyball games with our sweet-voiced, 6'10" power forward Julius Blayock, whose look and size led to his affectionate nickname, Baby Shaq. Koby and Arnathan made public service appearances at Coach Piper's daughter's grade school, Arnathan having replaced Baby Shaq, whose look and size frightened the children. Because of legal fees and alimony that dated back to the Reagan administration, Dennis had to work a part-time job at the Tyson plant in town, gutting chickens before practice, but he also had a work-study job, occasionally running a lawnmower over Coach's yard while DeWayne

144

manned the weed-eater, each of them taking several glasses of lemonade from Piper's sexy wife.

The varsity lived in two houses less than a block from the gym, six or seven guys to a house, plus two younger members of the coaching staff. The Basketball House had cable television and a phone line. Two bathrooms. Air conditioners in each room. Because of a snafu in the admissions office, I was assigned to the dorms my first day on campus and I didn't benefit from the air conditioning my first semester. Coach Piper kept promising that he was working on getting me moved over, but didn't have time for paperwork, practice season being upon us. I wanted out of the dorms for the obvious reasons—community showers, cramped quarters, unexplained stenches—and my status with the varsity team had also left me isolated among the guys I lived with. My schedule never matched their schedules, and I often ate in the cafeteria alone, unless Hubert had been too lazy to make the trip when everyone else had gone. Though no one came right out and said it, a sense of envy loomed daily, in questions about how practice was going or admiration for the Air Jordans I'd scored as my team shoes. Actually, my living companions were paying for my shoes, but thankfully, they never addressed vocally my trickle-down Air Jordans.

I can't say I was looking forward to the Basketball House, either. While years of saturating myself with black culture had opened my mind, the saturation perpetuated a few stereotypes, as well. Some of the stereotypes were realized and some weren't—it seemed nobody on my team liked watermelon—but all of these stereotypes inflated reality. Not to mention, I'd always witnessed these often glamorous stereotypes from the safety of distance in a Midwest subdivision. I'd never slept under the same roof as them.

Ice Cube lyrics about fucking up Whitey were more fun when I was the black man.

Nobody on the team fucked me up, of course. All in all, they were a great group of guys. Things got clearer as the months passed, and by the time I moved into the Basketball House my fear had waned, or been sweated away with my teammates on the court. But while I wish I could say I was shocked to find out how wrong I was, how every preconception should've been burned, that's not the truth, either.

In three years of driving in high school, I'd been stopped once in my hometown, doing eighty in a fifty-five. The ticket took a chunk out of my wallet, but in the end, no harm was done. In two years of living at Northern Missouri, I was pulled over six times, often for minor infractions. On each occasion, I was with a black teammate.

The first time it happened, I was incredulous, until, after asking, "What the fuck was that?" for the third time, Vance raised his eyebrows, grinned, and shook his head.

"Think about it, yo."

I was embarrassed, my years of studying the anti-cop lyrics of N.W.A. leaving me at that moment. "Oh," I said. "Yeah."

I made a crack about playing A.C. to Vincent's O.J., a crack we both laughed about after the cop returned my license. A few years after I left Northern, the crack lost its humor when Vance showed up on *America's Most Wanted*—the television show, and the actual list. Our cheap education and free tennis shoes hadn't gotten Vance very far in the real world, and he took to sticking up grocery stores and gas stations in the Kansas City area. He wore a golfer's cap and never flashed his gun. He used "Please" and "Thank You" and was dubbed The Polite Bandit. Once he'd used Mouton's name as an alias.

Baby Shaq took a fondness to me during ticket duty and at fall open gym, where a group of varsity guys were allowed in the gym for pick-up games. He stood amazed by my

146

strength in the post. He figured I must be un-human. "You been lifting them horses or something?" he asked, knowing I came from a small-town and figuring it must've been full of farm animals. He made an exaggerated lifting motion with his arms.

Baby Shaq also had a fondness for the ladies. Though I don't know the details, I heard that during the early months of my freshman year Baby Shaq was hooking up with a local crack dealer's sister. This dealer, a black guy named Augustus, actually used to play basketball for Northern—it seems that half of this town's minorities had played sports for Northern Missouri at some point—but he'd been ejected for dealing crack. He still had friends at the school, and held a grudge against the basketball program. There were rumors that he had it in for Baby Shaq for a number of reasons, but the most incendiary concerned Augustus's sister. This led to an ugly incident in the Burns Athletic Center a few weeks into fall practice, just days after the O.J. verdict. Though G-Funk's prediction of a full-scale race riot had been off the mark, an ugly scene of mob violence did come home to roost at Northern Missouri.

Burns was in the process of adding another gym, but for the time being, a rubber-floored court just beyond the varsity's main court served as home to intramural pick-up games. Coach Piper often let these pick-up games continue until afternoon practice started. The games weren't policed, and sometimes locals snuck in to get in on the pick-up action. Augustus showed up from time to time with a posse of three or four, all of them very good. On this day, I was on the varsity court early, working on my free throws. I noticed the game on the intramural court getting physical. Good-natured ribbing turned into verbal sparring. Tension rose, then backed away. When more of the varsity guys showed up, I shot turnaround jumpers with Anthony and Maurice.

Baby Shaq sauntered out of the locker room, dribbling a ball wildly and laughing it up with Koby, and he turned to the intramural action when he heard his name called. One of his pals from the football team had made a random comment, to which Baby Shaq grinned a toothy reply, and it was then that Augustus decided to throw in his two cents about his disgust for Baby Shaq. The intensity of the game still pumping through their bodies, the football player and Augustus began jawing, and this jawing soon included Lil' Mike, an associate of Augustus's from the Northern baseball squad. Baby Shaq walked toward the intramural courts. Koby called him back. Vance overheard something familiar and stepped to the edge of our court's hardwood. Coach Piper had made his way out of his office and started jogging towards what had turned into yelling.

I heard, "Motherfucker," but I couldn't tell who said it. I did see, however, what madness followed, street justice ready to be served on the soft rubber of Northern's intramural courts.

As coaches and managers sprinted towards the court and held back the varsity guys who'd wandered too close to the action, Baby Shaq wound up and fired the basketball at Augustus's nose. This was a close range blow, and the ball popped Augustus's head back, causing him to stumble and cover his face. Lil' Mike jumped Baby Shaq, who shook him off, and the football player tackled Augustus. The other intramural guys tried to break it up, finding themselves suddenly involved.

From a spot near our Viking emblem, on the left wing, I kept silent and watched six black men pound the living shit out of each other. It got bloody. It got sloppy. The brawl would last minutes. Our coaches and managers struggled breathlessly to restrain the varsity guys trying to help Baby Shaq, who was faring nicely with Lil' Mike, and displaying more power than he ever did in the post. An assistant wrestling coach happened to be in the gym and was able to use a few moves on the main combatants. Campus security showed up first, able to do very little with their walkie-talkies and books of blank parking tickets. The local police soon followed.

No coach felt the need to restrain me, as I stood in my place unguarded, cautious with marvel.

Over winter break, I moved into the Basketball House, finally excited for the big step, though the relocation was bittersweet, too, as I was moving into Baby Shaq's old room. He'd lost his appeal with the college council, and was officially kicked out of school a day before finals started. I shared the second house with Arnathan, Koby, Anthony, and Maurice. They clued me in on the etiquette of the house, letting me know that the only real rule involved the thermostat, which was to be kept at a consistent 85–90 degrees during the cold winter, seeing as four out of my five housemates' Louisiana nature couldn't stand the cold.

I had my own room, which I decorated sparingly, tacking up the *Sports Illustrated* covers from my old room in Maddox, as well as articles on our team from the local newspaper. We went on a six-game winning streak in January, which included a home victory against the number one team in the country. One of the articles featured a photo of me blocking a shot, and if you looked close enough, you could see my teammates on the bench standing up and cheering in the background. As a kind of joke, I also tacked a cover of *Newsweek* up, featuring a grinning O.J., post-trial. I'd glued on my own headline, though, letting it read "No Justice, No G-Funk," a riff on a sign I'd once seen during the coverage of the L.A. Riots. I tried explaining the joke to my housemates, but I don't know if they saw the texture.

I saw little of the guys I left behind at Maddox Hall, but sometimes Hubert came over to watch television with me. He'd already decided not to come back next year, and was just playing out the string with the junior varsity, anxious to attend classes closer to his home in St. Louis. When we watched cable, he was every bit as sluggish as he'd been in our old room, but occasionally he'd say, "Jesus, it's hot in here." I explained the rules about the thermostat. He nodded apathetically.

But it was really fucking hot. I often had to turn on the air conditioner in my window, despite the sub-zero temperatures outside my wall. Winters got brutal that far north in Missouri. In fact, the third weekend after I moved in, our area was blanketed with a snow and ice mixture that kept the town shut down for days. The night the front rolled in, the sky charcoal with chunky clouds, I watched lonely from my window. The yards and the ditches and the parking lots were wonderful lakes of simple white fluff. Undisturbed, for the most part. Even the eight or nine snowed-in vehicles I spotted at the Burns Complex's parking lot looked peaceful as they sat, not desperate. Near the Basketball House, there were a few construction areas, and, a few days earlier, passing by, I realized how ugly and polluted they all seemed. Why I thought of this, is anyone's guess. But I'd noticed the muddy pipes and metallic scraps and garbage and stacks of lumber and bricks and all sorts of large tools and machinery. There had been holes and pits near the ground surrounding the construction, holes and pits half-full of tan, murky water. There'd been trash and waste. The new building had been a pathetic skeleton of iron beams, fixed by a dirty concrete base.

Now the skeleton had some snowy bulk and muscle. Now the rest of the area was transformed and covered with white, connected to everything else, connected to all the rest of the beautiful white. The falling snow twisted and danced under the blast of the street lights. The bright ground contrasted with the dark sky. A landscape like that tends to blend night and day, giving everything an upside-down, glowing effect. It was one.

Meanwhile, I sat covered in sweat, discomforted, not unlike my first days on campus, my identity ready to melt away within the coming weeks, practices, seasons. I turned the air conditioner to max, and it blew noisily with confusion. Earlier that snowy evening, I had watched a movie in my room with Baby Shaq, who was sleeping on the floor of Maurice's room until he got himself set-up somewhere else. The other guys had traipsed through the snow to a party on the other side of campus, and Baby Shaq hadn't felt like tagging along, worn and beaten from a long day at Tyson, where Dennis had found him a job. The movie held our interest and laughter, and we talked about the upcoming week's rematch against William Jewell College, the whitest school in our conference and, because of this, our natural rivals. Baby Shaq had been in the bleachers during our upset, and celebrated with us at center court after the final horn had sounded. Still, I knew he was hurt not to have a part in it all.

Almost wistfully, he kept referring to Jewell as those "mothafuckin' white boys" and we laughed about their vanilla uniforms. Our Valley uniforms were baggy and brilliant, like the Michigan and Arkansas shorts I'd grown up admiring, myself once referring to a team or two in my high school conference as "those white boys." I didn't make this connection aloud, and though our conversation grew more and more relaxed in tone and language, we continued to scratch only the surface. At the same time, the closer I started feeling to Julius, the more I wanted an answer to this whole race thing. It felt easy, simple. Perhaps I might bring up O.J., in general, or Baby Shaq's menacing brawl with Augustus. Maybe I could mention the dynamic of a guy like G-Funk, slipping in references to my own mulattoed history of cultural envy. But I didn't, realizing that my head wasn't only vacant of answers to the riddle of race, but the questions, too.

I didn't want to fuck up the status I'd managed to create, so I mentioned something benign about the supposed 2Pac and Dr. Dre collaboration.

Later, Baby Shaq went back to Maurice's room, downstairs, calling it an early night, and nudging up the heat on his way. I cranked up my air even more. The air conditioner's racket competed with the Ice Cube CD I had spinning. I slipped out of my undershirt and stripped to my underwear. Cube rhymed about a good day he'd had in L.A., not even having to use his AK, and in my head, I rapped along to every last word, emphatic with the word "nigga." I continued watching the angry white flakes boogie outside my window, sitting Indian-style in my bed and then on the floor, alone and rich with the comfort of fake air blowing in my face.

PHOTOGRAPHS BY BRUCE WEST
In the Park

Trees by River

Oaks on Hill

Apple Orchard

Daylilies

A Family Photo Album

Writing and teaching writing—editing—don't necessarily get easier as we go along. So it goes with darned near everything. Getting older is among the ways we get dumber. But I'll not be stopped by the burdens of the experience. No way. I'll forge on today—and tomorrow—and the next day—but I'll be a good deal more circumspect, and more skeptical, and humbler. . . . I will not be less passionate, because I still believe in doing art and literature . . . . Hell, more than ever I believe that good art is good religion and that good art and religion are necessary for decent politics.

—James T. Whitehead, "The Bookworm"

Whitehead at home in his study, 1986
(Courtesy of Gen Broyles)

Nancy A. Williams

Walking with Jim

Neither of us could quite remember when we had started walking together, not the month or the year. When Jim died, I reckoned that we must have started our walks about eleven years earlier. Five mornings a week for eleven years he drove Gen to work, then swung by my house at ten minutes to seven, and we were off for an hour's walk around Gulley Park.

The land for the park had been donated to the people of Fayetteville by a family named Gulley, and it was still unimproved pasture when we started walking there, except for an asphalt path the city had laid around the perimeter. Meadowlarks nested in the long grass, and we saw scissor-tailed flycatchers, western king birds and bluebirds. A white horse on the Gulleys' adjacent property sometimes ambled over to the fence to be petted. This idyll lasted three years or so before signs of citification began to show up: surveyors and mowers, backhoes and pickup trucks. Our lamentations were ceaseless. Where will the meadowlarks live when they cut all the grass? What's that thing they're building over there? A gazebo? Oh, lord, spare us a gazebo!

Five or six other regulars were out at that hour; we greeted them but never joined them. A fortyish woman, who told us she was in real estate, greeted us cheerily as she zipped past. A middle-aged man in a safety helmet pedaled uncertainly on a bike too small for him, looking like the mama's boy we took him for. A strange, expressionless woman never made eye contact with us or responded to our good mornings, no doubt an axe murderer. Whenever I was out of town, Jim walked with a pleasant guy we saw every morning, and found out that he was a retired engineer. After a few years the pleasant engineer died, and Jim attended his funeral. He reported that the real estate woman had "cleaned up real well" for the funeral, and that the engineer's daughter had talked to the mourners about her insistence at her father's bedside that he get right with the lord before he died. Her account of trying to badger the dying man into heaven horrified Jim.

He was neither cheery nor zippy in the morning, thank god, but was patient and forbearing and steady. I wasn't required to be awake enough to speak until we were well into our 2.4 miles; he held forth in the meantime, no problem. When I think of that stretch of years, they seem a long banquet of talk: Bill Clinton's campaign and election, poetry, art, university politics, what's wrong with the NCAA. We sharpened our critical appraisals of the jogging styles and costumes we encountered. He insisted that I read Andrew Motion's biography of Philip Larkin, and I put him onto the art criticism of Max Friedlander. Walking loosens the tongue like alcohol—we talked, endlessly and easily.

Jim was a champion listener as well. When I was newly widowed, I must have bent his ear for weeks. He listened quietly, with little comment, while I poured out my heart. I could tell him anything. He never retailed anyone else's private affairs to me, so I knew and trusted his discretion.

He talked about theology. I remember little of what he said, not having a head for it. It seems to me now that his interest lay in the history of thought about the nature of god. I doubt that his passion for theology and philosophy translated into religious belief in any conventional sense, though he could be cagey about it. He relished his friend Bob Douglas's phrase about a man who became a minister of the lord: "he's in the religion dodge." Jim repeated the phrase I don't know how many times. He loved it.

We got into a row over IQ. When I said that no such thing exists in nature, he erupted. I stood my ground, relying for authority on Stephen J. Gould's delicious debunking of IQ tests in *The Mismeasure of Man*. But what good did it do me? "Goddamnit, Nancy, of course it exists." Jim's arms became windmills, his shouts carried across the park, his face turned an alarming red: I was witnessing a geyser of noble proportions.

Jim was rich in friends, and we talked about our friends a lot. What's Ellen Gilchrist up to these days, or Miller Williams? Jim relished his periodic trips to Mississippi to see his father and came back with stories about him, and about Tom Royals, Bob Evans, and John Little. He returned from one of those trips sporting a black satin windbreaker emblazoned with gold lettering: DUPREE TRUCKING, TAYLORSVILLE, MISSISSIPPI. The jacket's provenance included a detailed and convoluted history of the Dupree family.

Friends must never change, though. When a colleague announced his forthcoming divorce, the geyser effect came into play again, this time with the vilest execrations shouted across the park and into the neighborhoods beyond. The break-up of a family disturbed some deepest place in him. After my husband died, I was musing one day about whether I might move back to Denver. Old Faithful blew again: "Goddamnit, Nancy, you can't do that! Your whole support system is here. Don't be ridiculous!" "Those friends thou hast . . . grapple them unto thy soul with hoops of steel": I learned to feel cared for while being yelled at.

I told him that I was corresponding with a general surgeon in California whose name was Dr. Organ. Jim was a great appreciator of such stray bits of silliness—what could be better? One day he told me with some hilarity that his friend and colleague Walter Brown had forgotten to raise his garage door, and had backed his car into it, breaking it pretty

160

well to smithereens. When Jim died, Walter Brown arranged with the city to place a bench in Gulley Park in his memory.

After seven or eight years, Jim's feet started to give him some trouble, so we abandoned the park in favor of a more forgiving surface to walk on at the university track. There, we met up with John Harrison, retired dean of the university library, and Jim Jackson, a librarian at the law school. Until Jim's death, we four walked together every day. Three years? Four? Some resentment colored Jim's regard for John, dating from a crisis that nearly closed the University of Arkansas Press. John had been in favor of the closing; Jim vehemently had not. So, there was some tension, and our walks had an edgy feeling at first.

For the most part, Jim Jackson and I provided the audience; little was required of us but an appreciation of wit and general silliness. I do not know how John and Jim settled the question of which of them was going to lead this little pack. Certainly at the beginning there was a rivalry of sorts, unspoken, and maybe not a conscious one. How did they figure out how to get along? I could sense that it wasn't easy. They both were big, loud, profane, funny, intelligent, competitive, and successful men who, if they had been locked in a small room together, would have killed each other. I can say that the process took several weeks, though I can't describe it. As they worked it out, John Harrison ended up doing most of the talking in the mornings, and Jim Whitehead's job was to make the three of us laugh. I suppose plain civility on both their parts made our walks possible at the beginning. The edginess gradually ended, and we relaxed and gave up the rather too polite civility. As the months went on, occasionally I would see one old guy clapping the other on the shoulder with genuine affection.

We made few concessions to weather. If it rained, we walked at an indoor track nearby. Early mornings in winter I commenced my howl: are we having fun out here in the cold and dark? Why can't Gen retire so we can at least wait until it's light outside? But we never changed the hour. Unlike the rest of us, Jim Jackson had to get to work in the morning, and we wouldn't walk without him.

The circuit of the track took us alongside a huge scoreboard, which was made up of thousands of little lights. The lights were turned off, except for one tiny light that always stayed on. I said it was Tinker Bell, but the men were paranoid and said that "they" were watching us. One spring the scoreboard filled with birds, and Jim and John got into a big dispute over what kind of birds they were. I volunteered to research the matter, since I can't stand arguments over facts. I phoned Joe Neale, co-author of *Arkansas Birds*, who identified them as score birds, or, alternatively, track birds. Joe's authority carried the day and pacified the antagonists.

Jim took an early retirement, primarily, he told me, to see to the care of his elderly father. Maybe his own accumulation of years was on his mind, I don't know, but what amused him most during the weeks before his father's death was his friend George Garrett's phrase, "geezer sex." This was even better than "religion dodge," and he nurtured it with glee.

In the summer of 2003 Jim and Gen made a long drive from Fayetteville to Denver and Santa Fe. They returned in time for Jim and me to walk a couple of times before I, too, left for a vacation in Colorado. He had gone to an exhibit of paintings by John Singer Sargeant at the Denver Art Museum. I told him I would go there, too, and we planned to compare notes when I got home. I received word of his death while I was in Colorado. Later, I went to the Sargeant exhibit, I guess because I told him I would, but it was hard to see the paintings through my tears.

WILLIAM F. HARRISON, M.D., DONALD S. HAYS,
JOHN N. MARR, HAROLD MCDUFFIE, KATHLEEN
W. PAULSON, M.D., AND ROBERT POMEROY

Recollections

I met Jim Whitehead shortly after I enrolled in the MFA program in creative writing at the University of Arkansas in 1979. I had already read his poetry and *Joiner*, his dark, funny magic box of a novel filled with forearm shivers, moon pies, and theological disquisitions. In the years that followed, we became colleagues and friends. Each fall, we would drive to New Orleans to spend a long weekend, where we'd listen to the music, drink martinis at the Napoleon House, and, on Sunday, take in a Saints game. Once or twice a year, we drove to St. Louis for baseball games. We were there for the final weekend of Mark McGwire's magical, steroid-fueled season. We spent several spring breaks together in Europe—Paris, Amsterdam, The Hague, Prague, Munich, Vienna, Brussels, Bruges. Both of us loved painting, and we haunted the great art museums. Jim loved cathedrals, and we spent whole days in and around Notre Dame, Chartres, Mont St. Michel, and others. He knew the history of these cathedrals, could read the stories the stained glass windows told, the stories told by the carvings on the façade. He believed in God as an unknowable mystery, but he never gave up on his quest to confront that mystery, never quit asking himself how we should go about the daily business of living in the shadow of that mystery.

—Donald S. Hays

Differences separated us, though over the long haul they didn't amount to much. For one thing, while we were both Southern-bred, we came from different social worlds.

Jim came from educated, entrepreneurial-professional stock—his daddy had, I think, a masters degree in biology, and one of his grandfathers owned some sort of grain-trading business in St. Louis. They were prosperous, settled people. One also got the impression that they had social ambitions. He told me once that when he was young, his

Whitehead, published poet, 1966
(Courtesy of Gen Broyles)

mama enrolled him in an organization called The Sons of the Confederacy. She even bought him a little grey uniform with a red sash, although whether he wore the uniform and attended the meetings was never clear. For another thing, Jim had a good, solid education. Probably the first thing that I knew about him that truly impressed me was the fact that he'd gone to Vanderbilt University. Even though he'd attended on a football scholarship and, either before or after he got there, fell under the notion that God was calling him to preach (both were minuses to my mind), I had just enough learning to respect a proper education, and I knew that Vanderbilt was one of the places a person went to get one.

I came from more common stock than Jim. My forebears over the first four or five generations in America were undiluted Scots from the Inner Hebrides and the Western Highlands. They were an independent-minded clan, quick to take offense, quick to give it. They landed at Cape Fear before the Revolution and spread out from there, the branch that produced me descending across Alabama, into Mississippi, and finally into Texas. Well into this century most of them followed the plow, ran free-range cattle and hogs, and believed in free enterprise as though it were Holy Writ. We were taught from the cradle on that persons with African blood were the sons of Cain and that if a man belittled you, cheated you, or meddled with your women, you were obliged to humble him or kill him. Education was optional. Both my mother and daddy went to high school and believed that it would be a good thing if their children went on to college— it might allow them to open a store or a bank and build a house in town—but they also believed that it would likely spoil the scholar if they paid his way. So I joined the U.S. Air Force two days out of high school, and that was seen as a natural thing to do—a male came into his own by escaping his family's rule. America sent me to Châteauroux Air Base in France, where for the next three years, off-duty, I gained an education of a different sort. Home again in 1959, adrift, I wound up at Texas A&I, for no other reason than an old Air Force buddy said, "Come on down, I'll get you a job at this motel, we'll go to college." English seemed the obvious course of study because I liked to read stories and wasn't good at arithmetic. After a year or two, Bill Harrison (later, co-founder with Jim of the Arkansas Writing Program) showed up, and I became one of his acolytes. Adrift again in '63, jobless and broke, I signed up for four more years with the Air Force and was shortly afterward posted to Ankara, Turkey, where I again sought cultural learning opportunities. A civilian again in '68, just married, with no clear notion of how I was going to make a living, I settled on the possibility of attending graduate school and then, if that worked out, maybe teaching. Bill Harrison wrote back, "Come to Arkansas, I'll get you on." That's how, when, and where I met Jim.

I left the writing program in early 1971 without a degree, not having in hand a significant body of high-quality work to offer as a thesis. (Here, we shift briefly into the "nobody's fault" passive voice.) Harsh words were spoken, hard feelings harbored. That rift was mended long ago, and I only bring it up because it was the event that led directly to the deepening of my friendship with Jim.

Catherine and I bought a house and small acreage a few miles east of Fayetteville. She took a job teaching high school in Springdale, and I lied my way into a job carpentering, rationalizing that I'd soon finish a novel on the rain-out days and inside five years be hailed by reviewers and scholars across America as Faulkner's heir-apparent. We saw little of the old crowd for a year or so. Sam and Fay Gwynn came out, and we fed Leon Stokesbury now and then. Otherwise, it was life in the country. Then one sunny spring Sunday afternoon a van turned in, and Jim and Gen got out. Just happened to be passing. I don't remember that the kids were along. We visited awhile, and then Jim got to the point: If I wanted to finish the MFA, he'd chair my committee or whatever it took to get the degree. It was the kindest, most generous gesture anyone has ever made to me.

Jim was as good as his word. He greased the skids within the English Department and the graduate school, enabling me to fulfill the requirements for an MFA when, several years after he first offered to help, I decided I'd better stop screwing around and get a job teaching high school. In and around that time, too, he helped me to find an agent, and in a larger sense became chief lobbyist and sales manager for McDuffie, Inc. It was almost embarrassing to hear him push your case: You think, "Jesus, I ain't that good." But when the man believed in you, he was generous beyond description. I know of a half dozen others he did the same for. There are likely a hundred more I don't know of.

—Harold McDuffie

When you needed advice, Dad knew the right thing to say. During my residency training I used to tell him about the hospital politics, the chaos of patients' lives and about medical tragedies I witnessed, or as Dad would quote James Dickey, "the horrors of biology." I called him after I experienced my first obstetric death. I told him about the night a curly redheaded girl came by ambulance in her 8th month supposedly having an asthma attack. She arrived on a stretcher wide-eyed and sitting bolt upright gasping and saying "help me, help me" over and over. Her condition was obviously grave, but I tried not to show it. I kept on encouraging her. I tried to present some hope while we worked to save her. I stayed up with her all night, but by morning it was clear that she wouldn't survive. Early that morning we delivered her baby so that he would not die with her. At the end of that long day and night and day, I had to stand before God and all the medical students, physicians, and professors to explain her "case" and defend all the measures I had taken. They could find no fault with the care, but these teaching sessions are meant to find fault. One of the medical professors asked me what I had been telling the patient while we were preparing to intubate her. I answered, "Just keep on breathing and you will be OK." The professor looked over his reading glasses and glibly asked: "Well then, you lied to her, didn't you?" I picked up the medical chart on the podium and answered, "Yes, I did. And you are a bastard for saying so." Then I walked out of the room full of people. Of course, Dad was the first person I wanted to talk to. He listened. When I finished telling him what had happened, and what I had said, he replied, "Kathleen, you said the right thing. But now you have to apologize." I did, and the incident was quickly forgiven, but it was not entirely forgotten: I was later known as the only resident who had publicly questioned a professor's paternity and gotten away with it. Dad always knew the right thing to say.

—Kathleen W. Paulson, M.D.

One summer day—this would have been back in the middle '70's—Jim and Gen and some of the kids picked up Catherine, me, and our kid, and we drove to Blanchard Springs over close to Mountain View. There's a spectacular cavern there, and coming out of it some distance away a huge fall of cold, clean water that flows first into a swimming hole and then becomes Sylamore Creek. It has been a public use area going back to the WPA days. In more recent years, the Feds had turned it into a pristine park with first-class bath houses and picnic cabanas. Uphill a ways they had erected a glass and stone building over the entrance to the cave, and sunk elevators down into it; rangers wearing Smokey the Bear hats conducted tours on a clockwork schedule. We went swimming, then cooked burgers and weenies; the kids had quieted down; Gen and Catherine were packing leftovers back into the cooler. Jim and I were talking, probably about politics or the war. I remember that a silence had fallen. The summer heat was building; the sun glinted off the surface of the rushing creek; people were picnicking. Out of the

The Whitehead Family, 1974
(Courtesy of Gen Broyles)

blue Jim said, "Rich people hate this kind of place." The remark startled me. It was like a profession of new faith, a revelation. This from a man who mourned that his daddy had once turned down a chance to get in on the ground floor on the deal that became Holiday Inn; this coming from a man who countered the excesses of the far-left sentiment extant in the English Department by on occasion loudly and publicly giving Tricky Dick Nixon the benefit of a doubt.

Then there was the cloudy Sunday morning we were cutting wood on a place owned by one of my neighbors, an old Arkie bachelor named Earl Troutt. Earl lived back at the head of a hollow in a dark, three-room cabin that had been there since before his widowed grandma bought the place in the 1880's. Jim liked to go there. I think he believed he was getting in touch with the pure roots of America or something. He'd sit on the porch and bullshit with Earl, or if there was an excuse, go inside to breathe in the den-like odor of the place. The smell was a mix of wood smoke, of piss, of meat grease, of human bodies. But Earl wasn't home that morning; I had wood to split and haul. We were working across a spring branch running beside a lane leading back into the hollow. Neither of us saw the man coming along the track until he spoke. "I'm looking for an idaveline," he said. He stood across the branch, maybe a hundred feet away, a slim, swarthy skinned man with a close-cropped head. "What is it you are looking for?" I called. All I could think of was that an idaveline must be some kind of plant, but the fellow didn't look much like a botanist. "Idaveline," he said. His tone hinted at agitation. I recall wondering, what the hell is an idaveline, some kind of mushroom? "I don't understand what you are talking about," I called back. Jim leaned in and said to me in a low voice, "I think he may be looking for some woman." Instantly, I deciphered. The Velines were the branch of a family thereabouts who lived in a dilapidated single-wide with shed rooms built on and surrounded by a junkyard of derelict pickups, motorcycles, and bed springs with buckbrush growing through them. "I know who you are asking for now, she don't live this way," I told the fellow. I directed him to where this woman was likely to be. When he turned to head back out to the main road, you could see the handle of the automatic sticking out of his back pocket. After he was safely out of sight, Jim breathed, "That guy just got out of the pen." And he had. All that next week sheriff-cars prowled slowly along the back roads around our neck of the woods, hunting the guy, asking questions. He'd escaped from a prison farm over in the eastern part of the state. Jim loved it; he said his quick thinking kept us from getting shot.

And then there was the time we saw the buck drown. Jim had decided one fall that we needed to start fishing. So off and on for a month or two, he showed up just after daylight, and we'd go out on Beaver Lake, the impoundment that backed up White River for fifty miles. I had an old wooden boat and a nine-horse Johnson motor. We seldom caught a keeper. One particular morning we had motored a way up the lake where I knew of a ledge that I thought fish might favor. It was quiet, no other boats around. It was probably late October, cool enough for a jacket. We drifted a couple of hundred feet off one bank and cast to the ledge. You could see it down in the blue-brown water. The east bank was a half-mile behind us. A thin fog lay just off the surface of the water. Way off across the lake, a bell-mouthed hound bayed on a trail. Neither of us had gotten a bump, and I remember saying I thought we probably ought to move. The hound was louder. The boat had drifted sideways; I was standing up, casting; through the skim of fog, I saw something running the far bank. I said, "Look yonder, Jim, what's that?" You could just make out a frantic animal moving. Then the hound broke out of the woods over there, bawling every jump. Jim said, "It's somebody's cow." I told him no, it wasn't big enough for a cow. "It must be a deer." Whatever it was had disappeared in the fog. The hound bawled at the water's edge. After a minute or two we made out the deer swimming;

170

it seemed to be making straight for us. Deer don't swim very fast, and they ride low in the water, just their head out. Over on the far bank the hound was slacking off, losing interest. The deer labored toward us, slowly getting closer, maybe a hundred yards off by now. The dog hushed. Not a sound broke the silence. The deer came on. "It's a buck," Jim said. Sure enough, a four point, rags of velvet still clung to the slim antlers. A hundred feet out, it still had not seen us. "We need to move," I said and reached to pull the cranking cord. "No," Jim hissed, "You'll scare him." At maybe twenty feet out, the little buck finally recognized us as a danger. Its eyes were wild, and you could hear it fighting for air. At first, it looked as if the deer was trying to circle us. But no, it doubled back. Even going away, you could hear it moaning for air. There was no way the deer would swim the half-mile back. Nothing to be done, nothing we could do but watch. It went down even before we lost it in the skim of fog; the water boiled, then folded over it, and the surface went glassy. "Goddamn," Jim said, finally. Then, "goddamnit." I cranked the motor, and we headed back for the take-out.

—Harold McDuffie

Jim was one of the most interesting and complicated persons I have ever known. Extremely bright, extensively read on a wide variety of subjects, and a man of powerfully strong opinion. He was sometimes wrong but never in doubt. He was a very large man, strong as a bull and was prone to charge his friends and acquaintances like the said bull when they disagreed with him. But he was always a loving and generous friend to anyone in trouble and a favorite teacher in the writing program.

He loved to play poker with a group of friends. But he could never remember what a winning hand was. The first night I played with him, I thought he had stitches on his left hand, until I saw that the stitches were ink marks: HC for high card, 1 pair, 2 pair, 3 of a kind, straight, flush, full house,

171

4 of a kind, straight flush, 5 of a kind. Jim was a fine loser, generous, never getting angry at the winners, always polite and fun to be with. But he was the world's worst winner. Since he so rarely won, no one held his rare moments of unsportsmanlike taunting against him. And he was one of the best conversationalists I have ever known.

—William F. Harrison, M.D.

One of the main reasons I moved back to Fayetteville to retire was to be around Jim Whitehead. I admired his passion and intellect and I got the full force of both at our

Jim Whitehead, Bill Harrison, and
Miller Williams in front of Kimpel Hall, 1971
(Courtesy of Gen Broyles)

172

Sunday morning conversations over coffee. Because I was a professional airline pilot, Jim would defer to me on aviation matters. He somewhat deferred to me on politics and the American Civil War, but the rest of the subjects vexing mankind were his to explain. Typically, I would ask questions and he would give long verbal essays in reply. The depth of his knowledge was breathtaking and I knew that I was privy to something that few people, outside of his students, would ever witness.

Jim hated being called an intellectual so I refrained from calling him that, but I never stopped thinking of him as one. In the quiet of his living room I learned philosophy, religion, books, writers and poets. He was a master storyteller. I learned of the WW I cemeteries and cathedrals of France. I was given a first-rate tour of Paris with Jim as the tour guide. He told me of his adventure to the Amazon. He shared his history, of meeting Gen and Bill Harrison, of the early days at Vandy and starting the writing program. It was all fascinating stuff.

—Robert Pomeroy

Guest writers would stay at our house. I'd try to sit at Dad's right side where the conversation would be the best. As I got older I would stay upstairs for the parties, something Dad never discouraged. Once at a party I spoke with a writing student who mistook me for just another coed. When he realized that I was Jim's daughter, he stepped back and said, "What's it like being a daughter of THE MAN?"

—Kathleen W. Paulson, M.D.

We argued a lot, Jim and I, sometimes daily, often deep into the night. Sometimes our arguments were about practical matters, something to do with the writing program usually. But more often, we argued about literature, art, politics, theology. "Art and God," Jim used to say. "Outside of family and friends, what else is there?" Rarely were these arguments casual or academic. The truth is that it wasn't easy to have a casual conversation with Jim. He wasn't good at it. He didn't see the point of it. Oh, he could laugh and joke, and he was a generous friend. But he was, essentially, a serious man, not much given to small talk or conviviality. So our arguments, most of which took place on the little patio just outside the side door to his home, were fundamental to who we were. Jim was searching for a way of seeing, a way of believing or of accommodating unbelief, that could give shape and meaning to our lives. I'd like to think he found that before he died, but I doubt it. Like the best of us, Jim was too honest about such things, too fierce, to give in to easy solace.

—Donald S. Hays

When in an argument, Jim could get pretty mad. Twice he threatened to pick me up off his couch and throw me out the front door. And he would classify me as he did others. In one argument he said I was a priest. (He knew I had been raised in the Catholic Church, even though I was no longer a practicing Catholic.) As we continued the discussion, he said I was a bishop and then later an archbishop. I think that if we had continued that night, I might have been promoted as far as Cardinal.

He was ambivalent about Catholicism. One day he startled me by saying he was thinking about attending the Catholic Church, and then the next day he was going on about Luther being right. When the triplets were born, Catholicism was in again. He invited Father Bruce Street to baptize them and asked Jo and me to be the Godparents. All the children were there, gathered in a circle, including Bill and Merlee Harrison's three. Bruce baptized all ten children, and later left the priesthood and went on to get a Ph.D. and become a college president. We never believed the baptism was a cause.

Jim was not closed-minded or dogmatic. He could integrate new information into his belief system faster than anybody else I have known.

—John N. Marr

We were mostly afraid of him when we were small. He was so big. He was intense and loud about his expectations and even louder if you didn't meet them. By the time I got to high school I had figured out that I could disagree and even argue with him as long as I kept my tone and composure. Of course, it WAS intimidating to have Dad yell at you, but he would listen to anything you had to say as long as you didn't let anything slip that could be construed as impatience, disrespect or insolence. To raise your voice would be disrespectful, a sarcastic remark would be insolence, but tears—the worst of all—would be an attempt to get sympathy and was not tolerated. Keeping calm was the best way to deal with my Dad. My mother did that naturally, but I had to work at it.

—Kathleen W. Paulson, M.D.

Jim Whitehead was big, fierce, passionate. He possessed a deep intelligence that was incapable of glibness and almost incapable of irony. He was a dear but difficult friend, stubborn and sometimes unreasonably demanding. He was filled with contradictions. He could be stubborn, wrongheaded, bullying. He could be tender, generous, thoughtful. He was a magnificent teacher, an underappreciated poet, the author of a powerful, original novel, a lifelong offensive tackle who, fully suited, went after God as if He were a knockdown linebacker.

—Donald S. Hays

December 11, 2004

To dear Gen, a picture
of Jim taken in the
back of my house in
Madison, MS in
July 2001. He is hot
because it's hot, but
there's a fan up nearby.
Notice the pen in hand.
Look at his wonderful
concentration as he
reads my manuscript.
He is loved by many,
as you are, dear Gen.

*Letter from Charlotte
Mears Stovall, 2004,
accompanying the following
photograph*

Whitehead reading, 2001
(Courtesy of Gen Broyles)

Some will say that there are indeed passionate writers living in sacrificial poverty . . . .

One day in San Francisco, the novelist Herb —— was walking along with Jack —— and of a sudden began to tell his friend the poet how much he admired his work, and how much he admired how much Jack had sacrificed for his poetry.

Jack listened and was confused by what he was hearing . . . . But Jack is an honest soul above all, so he told Herb the bold truth. He said, "Herb, I've lived exactly the way I've wanted to. I enjoy the way I've lived. I've not been sacrificial if being sacrificial means the feeling that you've given up something you want."

Would Jack feel so go good about his life had he (his poetry) not been recognized? Surely not. But he would not change his life.

—James T. Whitehead, "The Bookworm"

Notes on Contributors

JAMES S. BAUMLIN teaches English at Missouri State University. He has published widely in fields of criticism, the history of rhetoric, and English renaissance poetry.

W. D. BLACKMON is professor and Head of the English department at Missouri State University. He looks forward to publishing his collection of stories, *Blood and Milk*.

VAN K. BROCK helped found the writing program at Florida State University. His numerous poetry collections include *Lightered: New and Selected Poems* and *Unspeakable Strangers*.

MICHAEL BURNS is emeritus professor of English at Missouri State University, where he taught creative writing. A graduate of the creative writing program at the University of Arkansas, Fayetteville, he has published several poetry collections, including *The Secret Names* and *It Will Be All Right in the Morning*.

JOSH CAPPS received his BA in creative writing from Missouri State University and his MFA from the University of Arkansas, Fayetteville. His work has appeared in *The Mississippi Review, Carve Magazine*, and other journals.

JIMMY CARTER is the thirty-ninth President of the United States and an accomplished writer, whose books include *Always A Reckoning* and *Talking Peace*.

JOHN DUFRESNE teaches writing at Florida International University. His books include the short story collection, *The Way That Water Enters Stone*, and the novel, *Requiem, Mass*. He is a graduate of the creative writing program at the University of Arkansas, Fayetteville.

JOHN DUVAL teaches creative writing and translation at the University of Arkansas, Fayetteville. His books of translation include Cesare Pascarella's *Discovery of America* and *Fabliaux, Fair and Foul*.

BETH ANN FENNELLY is associate professor of English at the University of Mississippi and is a graduate of the creative writing program at the University of Arkansas, Fayetteville. She has published four books, three poetry and one nonfiction, all from W. W. Norton.

178

JESSICA GLOVER has completed her M.A. in English at Missouri State University and looks forward to a career in teaching and creative writing. She helped Michael Burns select materials for *Common Need: New & Selected Poems by James T. Whitehead.*

ROB GRIFFITH is associate professor of English at the University of Evansville, where he teaches creative writing, and Associate Director of the University of Evansville Press. His poetry collections include *A Manatee in Plato's Cave.* He is a graduate of the creative writing program at the University of Arkansas, Fayetteville.

R. S. GWYNN is poet in residence at Lamar University and author of several poetry collections, including *No Word of Farewell: Selected Poems 1970-2000.* He is a graduate of the creative writing program at the University of Arkansas, Fayetteville.

BILL HARRISON is an emeritus professor and co-founder (with Whitehead) of the creative writing program at the University of Arkansas, Fayetteville. His many works include the novel, *The Theologian,* and the screenplay, *Rollerball.*

WILLIAM F. HARRISON, M.D. is a long-time friend and traveling partner of Whitehead's. He is a gynecologist in private practice in Fayetteville.

DONALD S. HAYS is associate professor and director of programs in creative writing at the University of Arkansas, Fayetteville. His published novels include *The Dixie Association* and *The Hangman's Children.*

MICHAEL HEFFERNAN is professor of English in the University of Arkansas, Fayetteville, where he teaches creative writing. His numerous poetry collections include *The Night Breeze Off the Ocean* and *The Man at Home.*

JOHN N. MARR is an emeritus professor of psychology at the University of Arkansas, Fayetteville, and a long-time friend of Whitehead's.

JO MCDOUGALL co-directed the creative writing program at Pittsburg State University and has taught at the University of Arkansas, Little Rock. Her poetry collections include *Dirt* and *Satisfied with Havoc.* She is a graduate of the creative writing program at the University of Arkansas, Fayetteville.

HAROLD MCDUFFIE is a graduate of the creative writing program at the University of Arkansas, Fayetteville. He is a retired high school English teacher and cattle rancher.

LEWIS "BUDDY" NORDAN is emeritus professor of English at the University of Pittsburgh. He has published eight books of fiction and lives with his wife Alicia in Sewqickley, Pennsylvania.

KATHLEEN W. PAULSON, M.D. is a daughter of Jim and Gen Whitehead and a physician in private practice in Fayetteville.

ROBERT POMEROY is a retired airline pilot and a long-time friend of Whitehead's.

ERIC SENTELL is completing his M.A. in composition and rhetoric at Missouri State University.

DAVE SMITH teaches in the English department at Johns Hopkins University. His numerous poetry collections include *Little Boats, Unsalvaged*, and *The Wick of Memory: New and Selected Poems, 1970-2000*.

CALEB STOKES is a high school English teacher who is completing his M.A. in writing at Missouri State University.

LEON STOKESBURY is a graduate of the creative writing program at the University of Arkansas, Fayetteville. Professor of writing at Georgia State University, his poetry collections include *Often in Different Landscapes* and *Autumn Rhythm: New and Selected Poems*.

BRUCE WEST is professor of art and design at Missouri State University. His recent photography documents the rural landscape and culture of the Mississippi Delta.

MILLER WILLIAMS is emeritus professor of English at the University of Arkansas, Fayetteville, and was the first Director of the University of Arkansas Press. In 1997, he read a poem at President Clinton's inauguration. His numerous book publications include *Some Jazz Awhile: Collected Poems* and *Making a Poem: Some Thoughts About Poetry and the People Who Write It*.

NANCY A. WILLIAMS is a long-time friend and walking-companion of Whitehead's. She edited *Arkansas Biography: A Collection of Notable Lives*.

C. D. WRIGHT is a graduate of the creative writing program at the University of Arkansas, Fayetteville, and author of numerous books, including *The Lost Roads Project: A Walk-in Book of Arkansas*. Her most recent collection is *Rising, Falling, Hovering*.

180

STEVE YATES is Assistant Director and Marketing Director at the University Press of Mississippi. His fiction has appeared in *The Ontario Review, The Missouri Review*, and other journals.

This book is a joint venture of the Missouri State University
Departments of English and Art and Design.
With series lists in "Arts and Letters" and
"Ozarks History and Culture,"
Moon City Press
features collaborations
between students and faculty
over the various aspects of publication:
research, writing, editing, layout and design.

Printed in the United States
215388BV00002B/1/P

9 780913 785157